MORE THAN YOU

Thomas DePetro

ISBN 978-1-63814-891-3 (Paperback)
ISBN 978-1-68526-406-2 (Hardcover)
ISBN 978-1-63814-892-0 (Digital)

Copyright © 2021 Thomas DePetro
All rights reserved
First Edition

All rights reserved. No part of this publication may be reproduced, distributed, or transmitted in any form or by any means, including photocopying, recording, or other electronic or mechanical methods without the prior written permission of the publisher. For permission requests, solicit the publisher via the address below.

Covenant Books
11661 Hwy 707
Murrells Inlet, SC 29576
www.covenantbooks.com

I would like to dedicate my first book to three incredibly special people in my life:

    Thomas Anthony DePetro—my firstborn
    Alicia Fae DePetro—my first daughter

    Holly Michelle—the love of my life

CONTENTS

Preface 7
Acknowledgments 13

1	Building a Great Organization	15
2	The Butcher, Baker, and Candlestick Maker	33
3	Whom Should You Hire?	38
4	The First Thing Learned	50
5	Proper Communication	55
6	The Art of Training	75
7	Safety as a Personal Value	102
8	Become a "1 Percenter"	109
9	Follow Up and Never Stop Communicating	116
10	Goals	121
11	Accountability	124
12	Rewards vs. Fear	135
13	Accomplishments	143
14	Overproduction	150
15	Ego—The Greatest Killer	159
16	How to Spot a Great Leader	174
17	Empowering Great Leaders	197
18	Group Leaders	209
19	Mentoring	212
20	Technology	219
21	Sales and Marketing	226
22	Leading the Good (People, Product, and Service)	235
23	You Want the Nuggets	239

PREFACE

I love helping people. Don't you? I love helping others go from not believing in themselves to realizing they understand what it takes to be successful. I have first learned this from being one of eight kids in a loving family. My siblings and parents were extremely helpful, encouraging, and supportive. They made me excited to live life every day. They showed me simple skills I needed to learn while growing up. They showed me how to tie my shoes, ride a bike, and look both ways before crossing a street. They explained to me how to treat everyone fairly and never discriminate since we are all human beings doing our best. They trained me how to properly perform household chores, like wash and dry dishes, sweep floors, dust wood furniture, clean windows, rake leaves, shovel snow or mow the lawn, paint fences, etc. I felt so accomplished after my family members showed me how to be successful in my task. It endeared me to them for taking the time to show me things I did not know how to do. Their training made me feel confident in who I am. Their training made me feel a part of the family.

I love when others whom I work with leave work with an excitement about how they feel toward their job, the company, society, and their family. They leave the workplace with hope and confidence and head home to share their joy with their family. I like helping others feel this way. If you have not had this feeling, but you have children, you will understand this feeling completely when you help your children grow. If you do not have children, but you have siblings, you understand this feeling when you help your sibling succeed. The feeling brings much gratitude and satisfaction.

I have had the pleasure of working for two corporations that were rated the number 1 and number 4 Most Admired Companies in the World by *Forbes Magazine* during the times I was employed. I have an array of experience from operations to training and R&D to sales and business development manager. I have worked in human resources; conducted workshops for safety and operations; been a sales representative, sales manager, and business development director; and owned my own business. I have never been less than number 1 in my operations. I was a manager in corporate America at twenty-five years young. I have been less than number 1 in sales just once. I have seen and worked with successful people and companies, and many of my mentors in these admired companies taught me valuable business lessons. This book will offer proven information in many areas, which is needed to be successful in business.

I realized how much this book was needed when I was off work due to needing a hip replacement. I found myself entering numerous businesses and spending optimal time observing employees' behaviors and company procedures. My natural inclination was to observe, analyze, audit, and listen. I spoke to numerous friendly and professional owners and managers from a customer's perspective. Once they found out I was not completely ignorant of what it takes to be successful in business, they began to ask "how" questions. I found that most of these owners and managers were never aware of some of the ideas I was discussing with them. They loved the ideas and wondered who else was implementing these ideas. They started to understand how they could get an edge on their competition, exceed customer expectations, and grow their business. They saw the value in the concepts for improving to become a robust company.

I wrote this book to assist others who wish to lead in business. The book was written with two people in mind: the current employee and the college graduate. I initially wrote this for the college graduate who desires to lead others and accomplish success for everyone. After writing the book and sharing the contents with those who listened, I realized it would help more than just the college graduate.

I recognized that this book could help the person who has been an employee but would like to begin his or her own business. Such ambitious people usually have many questions and do not know where to begin. They do not know who or what is initially needed for this venture. For instance, this person may include a physician who wants to know how to better their practice. I bring this up because

I have called on physicians who asked me about my college degree. I explained it was a business degree, a combination of marketing and management. They proceeded to tell me they wished to improve their practice and asked me questions about marketing, management, and general business questions. I was approached by not just physicians who were wishing to begin their own practice, but also by physicians who were already the owners of multiple physician offices. They were most curious and attentive on how to improve what they already had. I have also been approached by contractors (plumbing, electrical, and heating and air-conditioning), mine workers, small business owners, medium-sized business owners, upper-level executives, nurses, nonprofit leaders, and even church leaders. I have been approached by numerous people from a variety of occupations about how to get into business or how to improve their business.

I wrote this book to help. I want everyone who wishes to be successful to have a guideline or reminder of what it takes to be successful. It takes intelligence, money, faith, hard work, and people to be successful. How do you find, hire, interact with, and retain talented people? What do you have to have in place as a foundation for your future growth? What do you do with leaders?

You may find you have not heard of or experienced some of the ideas I am suggesting in this book. Ask yourself where your business is rated by *Forbes Magazine* or a business publication, which rates companies in America. Could some of these ideas catapult your company to a higher level?

I also found joy in recognizing the great people in my life who have helped me. I realized this book would allow me not only to acknowledge these great people, but also to inspire readers to want to behave like these leaders. The people I compliment in this book are typically retired or do not need the bump in reputation for profit reasons. They are accomplished and successful in business and life. Regarding the coaches I have used as examples, their success cannot be questioned. Some of these coaches are friends, while others are good people I have followed and look up to. They are respected by their peers and loved by their fans. In the case of my compliments regarding my son and daughter, they are just overall great people who care about others. I am another proud dad of my two children who have grown to be an outstanding teacher and corporate manager. My son and daughter (Thomas and Alicia) have done what every parent wishes for their children: to be a better person than I am.

I have placed a few warnings in this book for your career protection. I would be writing this book from the perspective of a CEO, but I have discovered one reason I have derailed this potential. I have found that you can hold those below you accountable, but do not do it to those above you. I have found this results in failure 100 percent of the time, unless you are blessed enough to have mentors like those I mention in this book. I have owned my own business, so I can argue I have been a CEO at one point.

If you stand for what's right in life, you will need to have a mentor navigate you through the dangerous white-water rapids you will face in business. You will be shocked to find that not everyone cares about the employees or owners of companies. Some employees only care about getting a pay raise or time off. Some managers will care only about their career, while others will care only about profit. Great people and companies care about both. I have yet to leave a company where the employees who worked for and with me have not called me to tell me they miss me. I have yet to leave a company where profits did not improve while I was there. Yet I have been promoted and fired from several companies. This book will inform you how to be successful and how to avoid being fired.

I have been an entry-level employee, union member, team lead, supervisor, manager, sales representative, sales manager, business development director, business owner, trainer, trainer of trainers, and board member of several successful nonprofits. I have also been the founder and president of two nonprofit organizations, which were both successful and accomplished their goals. I have worked as a supervisor or manager in human resources, operations, R&D, industrial engineering, and training departments.

I have had the pleasure to play three sports throughout high school, for which many of the coaches had a profound effect on me. I was blessed to play college football (my dream), lettering three of four years. I was even asked by my head coach to stay on and undergrad coach for two years after playing. During this time that I coached, I discovered my love of helping others succeed. One of the young men I coached went on to play for the Buffalo Bills in two Super Bowls (Mark Maddox is an outstanding individual).

I can also say with a smile how I am undefeated (2–0) as a head coach. I was asked by my classmates to coach our girls' powder-puff football team in high school. We won as juniors and seniors against tough and brutal competition, so I was beyond proud of all of them. Those girls were just as rough as the boys' teams.

I have worked in numerous industries, including package distribution, pharmaceuticals, commercial insurance, home construction, road construction, home health, transportation, churches, sports coaching, and tutoring.

Lastly, I have spoken in churches, manager meetings, workshops, seminars, to sports teams, at eulogies, and someday at my own funeral. I am still working on the logistics to the last one.

The common denominators for success I have found in my experiences are strategically placed in the book to help you. If you do not have experience in these leadership positions, this book will help you. If you have been a leader for a while, I believe this book will remind you of a few ideas you may have forgotten. Perhaps you were never taught these concepts to propel you to more success. You may even find this would be a good book for someone you know, someone who could use this book as a head start to face the many challenges of business. My hope is that you will implement some of these thoughts and behaviors to obtain success and enjoy those whom you work with.

The one area of awareness I am communicating to you throughout this book is this: *it is about more than you. It* is referring to achieving success for a business, relationship, a single goal, or even just in life itself. Combine your greatness with another's greatness, and you will see and feel the synergy of success begin. Now, add a third great person or a fourth to the group, and you will start to understand what it takes to be even greater. Remember, you are great, but it is about more than you.

Happy reading.

ACKNOWLEDGMENTS

I wish to thank the following people for making this book become a reality with me:

First, my Holly Michelle, who told me to be the change that I wish to see in the world by writing this book I've been wanting to write. Holly told me this while I was recovering from hip replacement surgery. She is brilliant and beautiful.

Second, my handsome son, Thomas Anthony, who responded very enthusiastically when I told him I was serious about writing this book and had the first several pages written. Thomas encouraged me immensely by reminding me of the different positions I have held and performed well. He told me he loved the manuscript and uses it. That was all I needed to hear.

Thirdly, my beautiful daughter, Alicia, who encouraged me to write the book and reminded me of the many successes I have enjoyed making the book worth reading. She told me she wanted a copy.

I wish to thank Jim Pons (friend and former bass guitarist with the Turtles, Frank Zappa and the mothers, and Alice Cooper). Jim read my original manuscript of my first book and said he liked my unique style of writing. This encouraged me with hopes other readers would enjoy the read.

I want to thank a dear friend of mine Richard Lawson for providing his home for me to write this book. He offered a ranch-style home with a bathroom directly off from the bedroom. This was essential while I was recovering from my surgery. It was a beautiful, quiet, and peaceful environment to write. Richard passed away before I could get the book to be published, but he was a critical person in its writing.

I wish to thank my three endorsers on the book's back cover for their willingness to read the manuscript and offer honest feedback before they knew if they would like the manuscript or not. Mark Murphy, Steven Thompson, and Jim Brangenberg are remarkably busy leaders who were gracious with their time. All three men are thought leaders whose feedback strongly encouraged me.

I want to thank Mark and John Jr., Davoli and Chris Sullivan of Metro Diner in Jacksonville, Florida for inquiring with me about the book and emphatically stating they wanted to know when it came out.

I wish to thank Nicholle Spadaro for her artistic interpretations to begin each chapter. If you ever viewed my art drawings, you would thank Nicholle, also.

I wish to thank all the people, some acquaintances and other strangers, who offered me encouragement and whose questions solidified the need for the book.

I thank all my former coaches, fellow players, employees, coworkers, managers, companies, and lifelong friends for shaping my leadership style and showing me what works and what does not.

I wish to thank my family. My mom and dad who are both deceased (Fae and Dan). They were beyond words for amazing parents.

My brothers (Dan, Mike, Jim, Pete, and Bill) and my sisters (Nancy and Peggy). You all formed me in some way to become who I am. You are in each word I wrote in some way.

I wish to thank Covenant Publishing for accepting my manuscript and bringing this book to life for all of us. They have been professional and patient with me during my research for the best publisher and through the publishing process. I have another book coming out, which I hope they will publish also.

Lastly, I want to thank my Lord and Savior, Jesus Christ. He made everything above this line possible. And this is only some of the infinite things He has done for me.

1

Building a Great Organization

Always put people first, for without them, there is no organization.
—David Sikhosana

The reason you are reading this book is you stink at one area of business or another. Your company is lacking in one or more areas, and you know it can operate more successfully in these areas than it currently is demonstrating. You have weaknesses in your business acumen, and you know you or someone else must run this area of your company more effectively. Read on and let's take a step-by-step approach to building, transforming, or catapulting your company to success.

For your company to endure all future trials and obstacles, it must have a solid foundation. This is synonymous to building a home, whereby a house must have a strong foundation, or it will lean over time and may eventually fall if the foundation is weak. Likewise, if one constructs a building, the foundation must be strong, which is often wider than the building itself as it stretches upward toward the sky. The concept of a strong foundation is fundamentally used in most everything we do, whether it is a structure, a company, sports, a community, or even our own physical body. So if you were to build a business or company, what is needed to establish the foundation? Perhaps the better question, who is needed to establish the foundation? I am going to suggest a concept to you, which may be new to you.

The foundation of your company is not outside of your building or company, but inside.

Jim Casey, the founder of the United Parcel Service Inc. (UPS), was asked in his later years how his company acquired greatness and success. Casey replied, "Determined people working together can accomplish anything."[1]

The concept I want you to understand: great entities are built from great people, and great people are the foundation of any successful company (Thomas DePetro-now).

Casey started the American Messenger Company in 1907 (name changed to UPS in 1919) as a service for delivering telegrams to businesses and homes. He invited his younger brother George to help him run the company, who significantly advanced the engineering of sorting methods only several years later. When UPS shifted its business focus from telegrams to parcels in approximately 1913, George was the first to design the roller systems for UPS and then, eventually, the motorized belt systems. These rollers and belts were erected

---

[1] https://www.google.com/search?q=jim+casey%2C+determined+people+working+together&rlz=1C1CHBF_enUS851US851&oq=&aqs=chrome.0.69i59i450.3481196j0j15&sourceid=chrome&ie=UTF-8

to optimum heights to reduce employee injuries caused by bending and lifting boxes and packages. The company also performed time/motion studies to ensure that the systems operated as productive as possible. From this small company in Seattle, Washington, that used bikes and runners (people) for delivery, a conglomerate was born that is still in motion today. Delivery methods now include airplanes, aircraft, trucks, ships, and computers, which is quite a growth process to admire.

The concept of composing a foundation of talented and caring people is the crux of success. It is the key ingredient to a prosperous organization.

If you want to build a business, creating this sort of foundation will lead to greatness and a winning culture within the company. It is important to remember the dynamics are greater than you are—they are influenced by each individual.

Another leader of industry whose name you may recognize is Sir Richard Branson. In the 1970s, he created a small record contract company called Virgin Records. Sir Richard jokes about the early years when he had to sleep in his car because he put every penny into the company. It is well known that Sir Richard grew this company to become outstandingly successful and is now a multibillionaire. From Virgin Records, he expanded into the airline industry and birthed Virgin Airlines. Having, again, acquired much success with Virgin Air, Sir Richard has turned his focus to philanthropy over the last decade. Sir Richard has been quoted saying that he understood early on, going back to when he began Virgin Records, he must hire good people and treat his employees exceptionally well for them to treat customers in a similar or better manner. He also recognized that the foundation of his company *is* the employees. Knowing this about Sir Richard, I can at least say I think like a billionaire in one area of thought.

Considering that some billionaires may or may not always be good people, unfortunately, it is important to remember to think like a billionaire in some respects, while questioning if you are still treating people right. Keeping this in mind, take a few minutes to ponder the following questions:

- When was the last time you looked for a new career or job?
- If you had a top choice, where would you want to work, and why would you want to work there?
- Have you thought about opening your own business?
- What is your vision? Where would you locate the company?
- Whom do you hire, and who is going to help you run your business?
- Do you join with a partner?
- How do you get the money needed to operate the first year?
- Do you advertise, and how much?
- Do you start hiring a sales force immediately or wait until certain profits are in place consistently?
- How much overhead or inventory should you carry, if any at all?
- Do you hire an IT person to start or wait until the business grows?

These and many more questions will enter your thoughts as you start down the path of building your own business.

The one person I can say, without hesitation, whom I respect and admire greatly is the small business entrepreneur who attempts to start and grow a business. I lived my dream of owning my own business. I quickly realized why one must have, besides a strong business plan, enough working capital available to infuse into a new business in its first year. The working capital allows you to cover payroll, since your sales and revenue will usually not when you first begin. To gain employee cooperation, it is highly necessary to pay your employees to help operate your business.

Two areas you want to take special care of your employees and not make an error: their paycheck and their vacation time.

Working capital also enables you to order product, pay for advertising, cover rent, and pay for overhead costs. It allows one to make mistakes, which you will make, and prevents your business from failing due to the mistakes.

I made one mistake before I even opened my doors. I did not realize that my decision to start my business during the spring season was four months too late. It was not until I called on schools and universities encouraging them to order my product and request my service that my mistake became apparent. Because schools made their budget decisions for ordering products and services in December–January, this lack of knowledge cost me valuable revenue and time. My advice is do not rush into opening your own business; the right time to start your business is when you have answered all the questions on your business plan and have talked to other business owners in your industry. Ask other business owners as many questions as you can before making your decision to enter the industry you are considering. To prevent coming off as a competitor, it may be best to speak with someone in another state. Ask them important questions and ask what kind of ineffective decisions they made early on and what you should know before entering this market.

When I graduated college, I planned to work for a great organization that matched my skill set. I had the conventional plan to work successfully for thirty years for a successful company and then retire. I wanted to hold different challenging positions and help make the company great. Looking back, I am happy I worked for a variety of companies, which helped me to meet and learn from many great people. It not only made me who I am, but has allowed me to help other people achieve success through my training.

Over the past ten years, I have spoken to and shared knowledge with small, medium, and large business owners. Many managers, owners, and employees of these companies told me that my perspective and information was new and useful. Having received such positive feedback over the years inspired me to write this book in hopes of helping others to either achieve or increase their success. The information I am providing is proven and lucrative. While reading through this book and/or preparing the initiation of your business, keep one basic concept in mind: it's about more than you.

I believe most people want to work for a great organization. Have you ever noticed how difficult it is to get into a great organization? Openings are rare, but when one is available, it is filled almost immediately. Lack of open positions in companies like these begs the questions: What makes these organizations or companies such a great place to work? Why do people strive to work there?

This book is designed to help you whether you want to own your own business or work as a manager for a company. If you are an employee, it will give your insight into the needs of your supervisor, trainer, or manager and will help you to understand and appreciate the people you work with. My hope is that you enjoy your work, the company, and its owner more thoroughly. Finally, I hope you will realize, regardless of whether you are an owner, manager, supervisor, or employee, it is about more than you.

I briefly mentioned that I had the dream to run my own business—and I did. When I get the chance to do it again, and I will, I will approach it much wiser and successfully than the first time. I will be better prepared and will begin with the proper level of working capital to fuse into the business when the opportunity arises. I will also demand that the company is founded in the appropriate location. Statistics show that 90 percent of new businesses fail within the first year. This is common knowledge in the business world. On the bright side, did you know that 85 percent of business owners who go into business a second time succeed? I can see why this is true based on my own experience. Having decades' worth of knowledge, I know better how to approach my next business smarter and with more financial backing. I will run it as successfully as I have run operations for other companies and nonprofits for communities.

Congratulations to the statistical 10 percent of first-business successors, congratulations for defeating the risk of starting your own business. The entrepreneur is the motor of the American economy. Those who are still in business have worked their tails off and have made good decisions financially. They risked everything when they took out a loan to follow their dream. They employ people whom they rightfully pay for their work, while the owner assumes all the risk. If you are an employee, approach your owner when the time is right and let them know you appreciate them risking everything to start their business. It is an admirable trait to be willing to risk it all and make your life, others' lives, and the local economy better. Successful owners tend to be the first to arrive to work and the last to leave. They often work after hours at home or at professional organizations, such as Rotary, Chamber of Commerce, or International Business Network, to grow their business. If you ask successful business owners about their accomplishment(s), I am sure they will give much credit to the good people who helped them. Rather than taking an individualized standpoint, they realize company success is not solely based on their personal labor but includes the efforts of others as well. Chapter 2 discusses the key people you need on your team to start your path to a successful business.

I have realized that what I love to do is help others by training them and showing them how to be successful. I enjoy helping others regardless of whether I own the company or I am working for someone else. When I had my own business, it was apparent to my employees that I genuinely cared about them and those on my team. They told me they appreciated me for listening to them. This does not mean I didn't hold them accountable if a mistake (or error) was made on their part, but I was willing to listen and help if I could. For instance, several employees feared making sales calls via the phone. I trained them to overcome these fears by instilling confidence in them, not by beating them down. I role-played with them until they felt comfortable saying what needed to be said in their own words. Eventually, this worked; and they became successful in sales, which they never thought possible. I also wish that my advice, extracted from real-life situations, in this book encourages and helps you succeed.

Organizations that are great places to work are typically at the top of their industry regardless of whether it's a profit or non-profit business. The reason being is they have great people working within and talented leaders with experience and vision running the organization.

Organization leaders follow two of the most important elements to achieve success: treating people with respect and improving the company daily. These people have a passion for what they do. Great leaders do not just "go to work"; instead, they "go to their passion," where they help others and make a living doing it.

Have you noticed that with the increase in media coverage on TV and the internet, those who accomplish what most of us consider great success or financial independence are looking to do something else? What can be the reason for wanting to change routes when they are already on a successful one? It is because they have become aware that life is more than individual accomplishment—it is about making a significant impact on others as well. Life is about more than you are. This will be discussed in more detail in upcoming chapters.

Great organizations do not just happen. They are the result of a talented person or persons with a desire to do something to better their lives *and* the lives of others. One of the key characteristics the leaders of these companies exhibit is the desire and habit of complimenting those whom they work with. Compliments motivate and instill confidence in those who work for them. Also discussed is how leaders hold a worker accountable until they succeed at an assignment; thus, accountability and compliments are equally necessary.

Think about a company, organization, or sole propriety that does not improve the life of the person who owns, runs, or works in it. Think about the people in the local area who are also positively affected by this organization. Think about a service, product, or nonprofit that exists today and who it helps. You will likely find that every organization in existence owes its existence to a person or group of people. This statement sounds obvious, but it is a critical point in understanding great organizations.

How did they do it? Jim Casey was a good person who had an idea to fill a need, which would also allow him to make a living. As mentioned before, Casey invited his brother George to join the business and work together, offering a great service and making each other successful along the way. As the parcel business grew, they hired friends who worked hard in respective areas and paid them well. In fact, one of Jim's philosophies is this: "If you want the best help to work for you, you have to pay them the best in the industry."

MORE THAN YOU

Think about this concept for a moment. When someone is the best, should they receive the same pay as someone who is average or below average? Imagine if you were going to need a surgery to save your life. One doctor had repeatedly proven that they were the best with 100 percent successful results (100 percent lives saved). Another doctor had repeatedly proven results of 50 percent success and 50 percent failure (50 percent saved lives, 50 percent deaths). Which doctor do you want to operate on you? Do you think both doctors deserve the same pay? If it is the same surgery, what makes one doctor more valuable than another?

Jim Casey understood this concept and realized if he wanted to attract the best service people in the delivery business, he would need to pay them the best in the industry. People who are paid well desire to stay with the company and do their best each day. Despite having the highest payroll, he managed to grow the business every year, even during the Great Depression. While his personal wealth increased and he enjoyed consistent prosperity throughout his life, the wealth, benefits, and lives of his employees also improved. In his later years, Jim realized that he wanted the managers of his company to manage as if they owned the company, so he gave them stock in the company as an incentive. He implemented the ideology "we are owned by our managers and managed by our owners."

Today, UPS still thrives and is a much-admired company. I consider UPS as the gold standard of how to establish, operate, and thrive a successful business. The culture created at UPS is real, and I have worked for other companies that could benefit greatly from following UPS's style. Jim later became a philanthropist with his wife, Ann. Their foundations have helped and still help many people. They have both since passed away, but their good work and positive influence carries on. Jim and Ann Casey understood the business's success was about more than them. To grasp true and lasting success, it is critical to realize life is more than about you.

I have applied to a few smaller companies, where the employers blatantly told me that their company "was not for me." Their reasoning was that I would get bored since their company was small, in case I had not noticed. Wait a minute, what? Are you telling me I cannot pass onto your people what great mentors of mine have taught me? You do not want me to help grow your company or create a winning culture? You do not want me to share successful and proven processes? I am open to your ideas to improve business and myself. These processes have helped these other companies grow to the top 5 most admired companies in the world. How would I be bored if you teach me what you know and show me how to lead your business? I will gladly train and pass onto their people skills I have learned from other great leaders. I would listen to others in their company and learn from them. Some get it, but others do not. It's about more than you.

This reasoning may sound like a joke, but sadly, I assure you this really happened—hiring managers and corporate trainers have told me I would not like to work for their company. It could be due to their unhappiness with the company; it could be due to insecurities about losing their job. Maybe they are just not intelligent, or they fear I will take their position. I really do not understand why someone would say this to someone, whom he or she viewed as having talent, to defer him or her from the company. It could not have been my attitude—that is one of the few things I have going for me.

I was taught by my friend and incredible mentor Bob Crouch that my job as a manager is to spot, attract, and retain talented people for the company. It is also my duty to train prospective employees properly. If needed, I will willingly move over or up to allow the person and company to grow. I understand that when the company grows, it allows me to increase not only my knowledge, but also my training, income, and benefits.

When sports fans hear the name Vincent Thomas Lombardi (legendary coach of the Green Bay Packers), they think of a great coach and champion. How many people realize Coach Lombardi brought great experiences and people with him from the New York Giants to help him succeed in Green Bay, Wisconsin? One such person was Coach Phil Bengtson, a defensive assistant coach with the Giants, who became the Packers' defensive coordinator. Early on, Phil worked as an assistant defensive coach under Coach and Defensive Coordinator Tom Landry in New York, who became the first head coach of the Dallas Cowboys in 1960, and eventually, a Hall of Fame coach. Anyways, back to the Packers—Coach Lombardi also brought Emlen Tunnell, the first black player elected to the NFL Hall of Fame, and Chuck Mercein from the Giants to become a running back for Green Bay. Chuck was designated as a key player for the historical 1967 Packers team, which defeated the Dallas Cowboys in the famous "Ice Bowl" game. To emphasize the effects of Coach Lombardi, he took over a team that had five first-round draft picks prior to his arrival and won only one game the year before. The Packers had good football players; they just needed a visionary, coach, and mentor to help them achieve greatness. Within seven years, Coach Lombardi led the Packers to five championships, including the first two NFL Super Bowls. In 1958, Dominic Olejniczak, the man who brought Coach Lombardi to the Packers, was elected as president of the Packers Board of Directors. Other credit is given to Jack Vainisi, the scout who recommended Coach Lombardi to board President Olejniczak. According to Coach Lombardi in an article published by the *Milwaukee+Wisconsin Journal Sentinel* (January 29, 1959), Vainisi was the only staff member retained by Lombardi from previous years. It takes good people to accomplish worthwhile achievements.

The concept that many good people lead to great accomplishments can be as it sounds. Leaders who maintain this concept, as well as their organization or company, will follow a consistent and successful path. One must remember to hire good people who have a desire to do the right thing and perform productively. It is vital that an organization must also invest in training, consistently follow up, and listen to employees. Measuring the individual success of each employee is the only way to hold them accountable and reward good performers. When you reward good performers, others will aspire to the same level of accomplishment. Companies must appreciate their employees by rewarding them in different ways and promoting those who demonstrate the ability to care for others and the organization. As a manager and/or owner, carefully choose team leaders who desire success for the organization or demonstrate the will to succeed. This does not necessarily mean to promote the person who is most productive all the time. As will be discussed later in the book, it means to promote the person who is the most passionate to obtain goals and cares for the people who are responsible for achieving those goals. Find an individual who will follow procedures and policies and appreciate those who perform the work daily.

I laugh when companies say, "People are our most valuable asset." Assets are items that are bought and sold every day in companies. Trucks are assets. Buildings are assets. Computers are assets. Inventory is an asset.

People are your most valuable gift.

People are made by God from God. We are helpful to one another because we each have a God-given gift. We are to use that gift to help others and the organization if we work in one. If we work on our own, then we are to help others in society by sharing or giving what we can with our time, talent, and gift.

I feel one of the greatest forces on earth is the "stay-at-home mom or dad." Do you want to know who works extremely hard for little or no pay or benefits? Do you want to know who treats the people under his or her care with the greatest compassion and passion possible? Do you want to know who can multitask, communicate several languages (that is, baby, dog, toddler, youngster, teen, and adult), meet a deadline, arrive to work on time, relate to other people in his or her position, communicate up the ladder and down, work with others in a team, start early and work late, work seven days a week, be always on call, never call in sick, train well, and be an expert in his or her field? It is the mother and father who can keep a smile on their face when there is no paycheck at the end of the week. Try to get people in your organizations to encompass just some of those qualities for no pay. Let me know how that works for you. Can you imagine if a business, nonprofit, or profit organization could get employees to willingly show all these qualities even with pay?

Therefore, I call the "stay-at-home moms and dads" the greatest, hardest workers on earth. They work rigorously for reasons other than pay, promotion, and career success. They do it because it is their gift from God. If a parent hears their calling, they recognize their gift and answer the call. They realize the importance of raising each child lovingly. Parents live their passion of nurturing every day, whether they acknowledge it or not. I am not saying all parents are the perfect example of hard workers. In fact, too many people focus on the weaknesses of others and overlook their unbelievable accomplishments. Remember to encourage, not discourage. We need to lend a hand, not point a finger.

I now want to discuss how an organization can accomplish greatness all while handling the challenges of paying employees, allowing them to rest and go home, producing a product or service, paying expenses, still bringing in revenue, and then using any leftover profit to put back into the entity.

Greatness begins with you, the leader. You must exhibit at least a few strong personality traits. You must be driven and willing to lead others. You must be solid in time management techniques. You must be analytical. You must keep your finger on the pulse of the company by developing and reading reports (later, I will name a few reports, but this is not an all-inclusive list). You will need to watch time card reports to make sure you are not paying too much in overtime, but not paying benefits to someone who is working too few hours per week. You will need to review your employee list to see how many employees are working as well as new hires, terminations, disability, quit, etc. If you are planning to grow, do you have enough employees?

You will need to review your accident and injury report. You will want to follow up with the areas where accidents have occurred and make sure your managers are retraining these people the very next day if they are not on workers' compensation. You want to make sure every manager calls his or her employees weekly if they are on workers' compensation to ask if they received their check. Also, ask how they are feeling. Not only will this make the injured employee feel appreciated, but they will also come back to work happy and loyal.

You should review your service report daily. Did you have any complaints? Did you make good on your service commitments? What did you sell or service and how much?

You will need to review your P&L (profit and loss) statement monthly. This will tell you what is trending for your expenses, revenue, and profits. You will want to have your managers send you their weekly planners. This way, you will know where they're spending their time and if they need to spend it somewhere else. You will want to read what is going on with your competition. Keeping up with legislative news about your industry will be important as well. I discuss later in the book why technology is vital to a company's success. You will want to read up on the latest R&D in your business or in a similar industry, which you can adapt to grow revenue and reduce expenses.

Remember, either you should know, or your assistant should remind you the anniversary date(s) that an employee(s) joined the company at the beginning of each week. You can send that employee a card, call, or e-mail them. This helps to establish just one great aspect of the culture within your company. Again, you can see there is a lot you have to analyze, which is why the people you hire are so critical to your success. You cannot do it alone; it is more than you. There just is not enough time for you to lead, mentor, and train every day. Additionally, I have not even broached the topic of visiting your customers and prospects.

Many of the examples I am going to share are from my personal experiences over thirty-five years in the business world. I have experienced both great and not-so-great companies, nonprofits, and churches. I have seen great, inspirational families that were worthy of sharing via movies or books, while others were train wrecks. I have felt the effects of tall egos, poor skills, wrongly promoted people, lack of caring, selfishness, and many other bad qualities that can ruin a family, organization, or church. I admit there were times I was the one guilty of these ill effects. Every day, people tell me many companies are not what they used to be. Employees do not feel trained, cared for, or respected. At the same time, company owners and managers tell me employees are not what they used to be. The managers do not feel employees care or respect them. On the other hand, I have had employees and managers tell me they appreciate my training ability, care, and respect. Therefore, I am writing this book. As wisely stated by Gandhi, "I am being the change I want to see in the world."

MORE THAN YOU

 I am going to shoot it to you straight and tell you the reality about people, including myself. I am not here to please you; I am here to make a positive difference in you and in the world. I will not use real names of people or organizations in negative stories, but the stories are real, and so are the successes and failures. I will use the proper name of a person or company in a positive story because those people and companies deserve to be mentioned and appreciated.

 If I can help or influence just one person who owns or runs an organization, this will push the wheels into forward motion toward reestablishing the habits that made this country the greatest in the world. I know success will then follow. *It starts with recognizing how your people, employees, and/or family are a gift from God.*

 I do not care who your god or higher power is, right now. I do not care if you're part of one of the major religions of the world or if you have your own philosophy. I am not concerned if you believe there is no God, and you oversee your own fate. I am not interested in arguing about what is right or wrong, explaining who God is, or pushing my beliefs—I do not want you to miss the point. If you believe people evolved from apes, then go and kiss the biggest ape you can find and thank them (tongue in cheek). Those who are Christians, Jewish, or other faiths might wonder why I do not care about who someone's God is. I know who my God is, and we talk throughout each day. Remember what God promised: seek and you shall find. What I care about, for the purpose of this book, is that you recognize all people are a gift. When you grasp this idea, you will change your world for the better. The concept to keep in mind is that it is about more than you.

 I would like to share my belief with you in hopes that my insight might make your efforts more successful working with others. I have had my peers approach me and ask me how I accomplished something. I explain to them in detail. I answer their questions, yet when they attempt to follow my methods, they are less successful. Why is this?

 First, I feel it is because they are trying to complete the success without genuinely caring for those whom they are working together with. It is like following the dance steps without listening to the music. It is not impossible, but it is much more difficult and less fun. You must genuinely care about those you work with in order to want to train them well, listen to their difficulties on the job, and help make them successful. It all starts from genuinely caring about others. You may find this difficult because you work in a large city or you work in a large company, which makes it difficult to get to know people more personally. Pretend you are someone else and this person is your sister, brother, mom, or dad. How do you want someone to treat your loved ones? Just remember, we are all the same inside our hearts. We have similar fears, goals, needs, etc. Most people fear being fired. Most people want to be successful at work. Most people want to be thought of kindly or respected. Most people need to pay bills, which is why they need a job. Once you understand most people want to be treated the good way you want to be treated, it opens a communication that allows you to show the other person you want their success also. Once this is communicated and shown, the trust begins to build. At this point, all you must do is guide the other person; listen to their thoughts, which may help you and the company; compliment them on work or ideas they do well; and explain to them when they are missing the mark. Explain how and why they are missing the mark, if they miss it, and gently guide them back to doing work successfully.

I find this easy due to my belief in Jesus, my Lord and my God. If we believe God made us to have a relationship with Him and our fellow person, it makes it easier to follow the simple idea of "treat others as you would like to be treated." If you believe in God, then you will notice He made more than one person on this earth. Don't you suppose He made us to work together, since it is so much easier to accomplish most everything with more than one person?

Once you try the idea of explaining to someone that you want to know what their goals are so you can help them achieve them, inside or outside the company, and you see how they respond to you, all the ideas in this book will begin to make sense. When you notice after a short time the other person is approaching you with ideas of improvement for the company, you will understand how they want your success and that of the company. Once you hear an employee give you an idea you have not thought of or reach out to an employee and make them better when you did not have this same effect on this employee they're helping, you begin to realize "it's about more than you." When you see one of your employees thank you for their check on payday and leave with a smile, you must follow this thought further. Imagine this person walking through the door where they live and smiling with their loved ones. They tell their loved ones they got paid and want to do something nice for the family. When I was young, my parents would tell us kids how they were taking us out for an ice cream cone to celebrate payday. It may seem like a small thing to you, but it was a huge treat for us as kids, and it made us amazingly happy. Now do you see how making a company successful is about more than you? It is about everyone you work with, including your family as well. It is about the customers smiling when your company made them the product or offered them great service. You affect so many people in this world in a positive or negative way. That is why we must always remember it is about more than us.

Have I ever gone to work sick, unhappy, tired? Sure, but you remember that you can have a positive effect on someone else, and it somehow gives you more energy. It gives me more purpose at work. How do you deal with the employee who appears to abuse drugs or alcohol? You send them for a drug test. Depending on the result of the test, you may have to wave them from your team. You cannot allow them to hurt himself or herself or another employee. How do you deal with an employee who is never happy? Have you sat down and explained honestly how you feel about them? Remember to start positive and talk about something they do well. Then talk honestly and tell them how you feel like they are never happy at work and complain a lot. Listen to what they are telling you regarding their cause of so much complaining. If you can fix it, do it. If you cannot fix it, explain why you cannot. Then end positive and give them some hope going forward. I explain this method more in chapter 5.

Don't you want someone to listen to you when you are frustrated? Don't you want someone to congratulate you when you do well? When you have a great idea of how to improve the workplace, don't you want someone to care and ask you about it? Are you doing this for others? If you are doing this for others, you are a leader. If you are not doing this for others, you do not understand that it is about more than you. You do not understand God's design.

Whenever we build something worthwhile, we want it to last; we want it to stand the test of time and become successful. Perhaps we desire this "something" to become the benchmark to which all other similar projects are compared. Before we build this "something," we must organize our thoughts and goals into a formal plan. Today, there are differing views about a piece of the puzzle to use as a foundation for your company. It is called the business plan. A business plan is an excellent tool for new or inexperienced entrepreneurs to construct and establish ownership of a new business. This sort of plan acts as a tool to help you conjugate ideas that have not yet been considered or do not have a solid written solution. Any bank or financial institution will demand that you provide a completed document or packet containing information of the plan prior to offering you a loan to establish your business. Although a business plan can take up to six months or longer to complete, it is necessary to have a better chance at success, in my opinion. I highly recommend you take this step seriously—plan your work and work your plan.

2

The Butcher, Baker, and Candlestick Maker

The butcher, baker, and candlestick maker have been around a lot longer than supermarkets and Wal-Mart.
—Joel Salatin

I approached Rudy after a church service one morning with the expectation of exchanging a quick hi. I was a young twelve-year-old boy and had hunted with Rudy a couple of times. He was my dad's friend since the 1920s and would call my dad on occasion to go hunting. Whenever Rudy called the house, I always immediately knew who it was by the tone and kindness of his voice. When I answered, he would politely introduce himself and say, "Hi, Tom, this is Rudy." He and my dad were cut from the same cloth in their humbleness and attitude. Rudy enjoyed the simplicity of getting out in the woods with an old friend and hearing my father's dogs bark when they spotted a target. My father hunted as well, but getting game was not as pertinent to him as it was to Rudy. I always enjoyed Rudy because he was soft spoken and kind. He was liked by many, young and old. He was what I would call, looking back, a gentleman. He often complimented me and told me what a good person my dad was to him and others.

As I approached Rudy after church this morning, a few well-dressed men, whom I did not recognize, were also walking toward him. Rudy said hello to me with his typical kind smile and soft-spoken voice, shook my hand, and asked how I was doing and if I was going hunting anytime soon. The other adults were not as courteous as Rudy, as they talked over me. They were quick to ask when he was going to stop by and how his land was doing. Rudy made sure to say it was nice talking to me before he turned his attention to the other men. I did not know Rudy had any land; I only knew he owned a home on top of a large hill in our town. It turned out Rudy owned more than just the land his home sat on. He owned all the acreage on the hill, which he developed into many lots, and the land below, which was turned into a trailer park. I later asked my dad about the other men who approached Rudy, whom he identified as a banker, attorney, and accountant. My mom, with her quick wit, quipped they were the butcher, baker, and candlestick maker. It made me laugh.

Some years later, I read a book by a self-made millionaire. He spoke of the time he was a boy and wanted to speak to the man he worked for. Before he could speak with his employer, he had to wait behind three men. Later, he asked his employer who those three men were. The employer stated that those three men, his banker, attorney, and accountant, whom he meets with weekly, are critical to every business owner. The employer in this book owned a construction company, grocery store, and buildings, among other large assets.

When I opened my business, I quickly found out the banker and accountant are particularly needed and important. The idea behind consulting with them is to prevent you from making mistakes. These people can help you proactively make the best decisions for yourself and your business's success.

An accountant will help you with reports, which show you where your greatest expense exists. This will allow you to look it square in the face and decide if you need to change something you are currently doing. The reports will show you where your greatest revenue is coming from, and from there you can decide if you want to continue this process or enhance it. The reports from your accountant will show you all the large and little expenses, from which you can decide if you can accomplish the same results with a different vendor or provider. They will also show if you need to cut back or add to certain aspects of your company. You will learn if your people are working safely or not. If not, you will understand the costs associated with their unsafe practices. They will reveal if your managers and employees are working productively. You will see your cost of service and determine if your pricing is adequate. You will learn to become more analytical from working closely with your accountant. There are times you will decide to hold off on an action due to your financial picture. The most obvious reason you need a good accountant is to ensure your taxes are done properly and legally. The tax laws change year to year, so you need a professional who knows what those changes are and how you can benefit from them. Many businesses have been shut down because they did not pay taxes. You will be surprised as a business owner to learn the various taxes that exist in business today. There are property taxes, inventory taxes, health benefit taxes, payroll taxes, and revenue or profit taxes, just to name a few. This will not happen if you begin your company with an accountant who works with you starting on the day you initiate your business plan. There may be times you will achieve a large order and decide to proceed, even if you do not have the money to purchase the needed product or material. This is where the banker comes in.

Your banker is someone who has a stake in your success. They want you to be successful because your failure means loss of revenue and profit for them as well. You can turn to your banker and provide evidence of why they should loan you money to fulfill an order or purchase something for the company. They can help you overcome obstacles you may face as your company grows. I assure you dire situations will arise that you did not see coming. The banker can help you with advice or money, whichever is more profitable. Because bankers have usually worked with many business owners, they can tell you where others have succeeded or failed. They can tell you how if your decision plan is a good idea or a recipe for disaster based on lessons learned from past business owners. As they are still human, your banker will not be right 100 percent of the time, especially if there is something new in your product or service that they had not dealt with before. However, they can offer a good barometer of how your idea may result.

Before starting my own business, I owned a trademark, so I needed a copyright/patent attorney to help me apply and proceed with purchasing the rights. I recommend finding an attorney who can be available when necessary and to develop a trusting relationship with him or her. It is pertinent to understand that we live in a litigious society. Your attorney can prevent you from making a decision that may place your company in the crosshairs of a person looking to profit from your mistake. Again, advice from a proven professional before you make the final decision is often necessary to prevent substantial loss. Many people will see your company name on a product, service, or fleet vehicle and assume you are a wealthy business owner. It does not matter to them whether you started the business yesterday or one hundred years ago. Some people will view your company as their means to earn money through the avenue of taking you to court. They wish to gain from your ignorance, negligence, or accident. Having a trusted and knowledgeable attorney on standby will protect you from further loss or damage to your company. If you are ever litigated against, a good attorney can offer wise counsel on whether you should settle or follow the judicial process if you are in a dispute. They can also suggest how to use the law to your advantage for your company. Thus, it is vital to develop a relationship with the attorney and heed their advice.

The butcher (a.k.a. the banker) provides the "meat" or funds. You will likely need money at some point in your business journey. The baker (a.k.a. the accountant) uses a precise formula to make a "cake" or make costs fit together. The candlestick maker (a.k.a. the attorney) will shed light on laws and make sure things run smoothly so things do not get out of hand and go up in flames. The attorney can make your life much smoother as you navigate the turbulent rivers of business ownership. The information and lessons you learn from these professionals will make you a wiser decision maker. Eventually, you will lean on them less for their advice as time goes on. However, early on, they are priceless. Lastly, but not least, remember these are relationships. Like any relationship, the more you put into it, the more you will make friends and enrich life for all of you.

3

Whom Should You Hire?

Great vision without great people is irrelevant.
—Jim Collins

The first midlevel manager, Bob Crouch, I met was at the first company I worked for out of college. As I recall, he firmly shook my hand and welcomed me to the company. He was dressed very professionally in a sharp suit and paisley tie. He smelled strongly of expensive cologne, and his hair was styled tightly with gel. His shoes were polished and shined. They looked like they were just taken out of the shoebox. Times were different back then—in 1986, people were not afraid to overgel their hair and douse themselves in perfume or cologne. I thanked him for hiring me and told him I would learn quickly and strive to be number 1. He told me he had all the confidence in the world that we would be the best. He was quick to assure me that he knew I was a good person and ambitious worker, which is why the company hired me. Later, Bob shared something with me that I will never forget:

"My number 1 job in this company is to spot, attract, and retain the best and most talented people available for our company."

Deep down inside, I wanted to enlighten Bob on how service was the most important aspect in business. I wanted to tell him I knew something was missing, preventing the company (or business) from advancing. Nevertheless, I held my tongue. He appeared highly successful, and I simply and wisely shook my head in agreement. He then explained his belief that everything else would fall into place *if* he and the other managers continued bringing success to the table. I thought about his point of view for a moment, going over all the things that make a company successful (profits, service, production, safety, accounting, computers, etc.) and realized Bob was right. Talented people make all the difference in all these areas. I wondered, does every company acknowledge this concept, and does the management execute this principle? I will cover more great ideas Bob taught me in upcoming chapters.

Today, many companies use software programs to weed out the employees they feel would not equate to success in their business. If it works, I think it is a great idea. However, remember one thing: the person you are weeding out might not be the right person for the job you posted, but it does not mean they wouldn't be good for another position in your company. An example would be if a company looked at both my resume and my personality for engineering, I would be kicked out of the applicant pile immediately. I have a well-rounded background in business in several disciplines, so I know I have an advantage over other candidates for a position in operations management, training, sales/sales management, or safety leadership. I also have the natural ability to train others. Training requires sales, management, listening, patience, knowledge, relating, leadership, speaking, understanding, and, most importantly, *caring*. I have an excellent record in operations management and have never been ranked less than number 1 in any operation of a company. This accomplishment of mine is not just because of me, it has been attained because of *us*—my management, my team, my employees, and my God. It is more than I am.

You should always look to hire the person who has the skill set and personality of a leader. Caring is one of the most important characteristics of a great leader, but remember, caring is not always a teachable trait. The way to find out if a person is caring is to ask them what they care about most. If it were money, they would be a great fit in commission sales for your company. If they were to speak of the people in their life, then a position in HR may be a good fit. Others may speak of how they improved processes in another company and the enjoyment they received from this. This person may be a great fit on your management team. Leaders who care about people will speak of how they have helped others to further their careers. They will speak of help others develop to better the company and protect or take care of the company by working with those within. Some may speak of how they enjoy volunteering at a specific charity. If your company has a position that oversees employees who volunteer at charities, this person may be a good coordinator or company liaison.

The prospective hire could still be halfway through college, be about to graduate, or have only recently graduated. This person may have demonstrated great abilities with another company, so you want them to work for you. This person may be more experienced in your company than most but has the desire to help others and share knowledge. This person might be at least old enough to understand how to treat people properly and still care. Asking the accurate questions is the key to finding out who the perspective employee is as an individual and if they are right for the position you are hiring them. You need to find out if this person cares about helping others. Remember that leaders give, and nonleaders take.

MORE THAN YOU

I have an elder brother, Bill, who used to take me to play two vs. two football against his friends. I was six to ten years old, and my brother and his two friends were four years older. My brother told me we could beat his two friends, our competition together even though I was younger and smaller. He would compliment me when I made a good play and tell me not to worry about it when I did not. He would explain and show me how to make a better play whenever I did something wrong. He kept motivating me to keep trying and not give up. He would scream praise of joy when I made a touchdown or an interception. He was always encouraging, and he was willing to work harder to cover for my lack of talent or ability when I was young.

This is what a leader does. They believe in you. They encourage you. They help you to get better with a caring attitude and show you how improve your ability to perform tasks. A leader screams praise when you do something correct or good, and if you make an error, they tell you not to worry and retrain you to do it properly. Leaders are competitive and do not fear a challenge. In fact, they invite challenges, as they know competition will test their abilities, which helps to learn what they are doing well and what they need to improve. As an example, my brother was my leader who helped me develop mentally and physically in our youth. Not only did I grow, but my speed and talent increased as well because of him. His training came to fruition when the two of us began dominating his friends in football games. His friends finally stopped accepting the two vs. two challenges from us. What my brother did for me is what businesses must do with employees. However, I recognize how my brother helped me learn and grow, but in return, he was able to win more and enjoy the smack talk or pride after the games due to helping me grow. Remember, it is about more than you. This is a key to business.

The first thing you must decide is what kind of employee you want to work for/with you. Why do you want them? What do you want them to do? Who will they be working with, for, and above? Do they need to have the desire to move up? Can you train them on the required skills? Do they need to already have these skills before joining us? Do they have a passion for what they do? Is money their primary reason for working?

Many successful people envisioned their dream before it became a reality. They saw it before it became a formal idea with a plan and design.

> Imagination is more important than knowledge. (Albert Einstein, *Cosmic Religion: With Other Opinions and Aphorisms*, 1931)

This is how a company should approach the next person they are hiring. The vision needs to be set with the department head, or the person who is going to be working with this new employee, and the person doing the hiring. An understanding of whom the next hire should be accomplished first, then the hunt to find this person can be executed.

I have seen companies I have worked for hire someone without ever talking to the person who must train them, work with them, communicate with them, or engage with them in some manner. These are not small companies but are some of the largest in the world and some of the most successful. Considering this, the obvious question arises: why change if the company is so successful? They must have done something right to grow to this point. When I brought up this question to former hiring personnel, they told me the respective company's hiring process changed from what they followed in the past. This is a big *red light*. So the company grew and became successful, but now the way of hiring people also needs to change?

When I was a young operations supervisor, my upper-level manager told me we hire good people; and if they fail, it may be due to my training or lack thereof. I spent a lot of time training the new employees and made sure to follow up with them by observing and listening to them. Sure enough, my manager was right—the new employees turned out to be successful, and I developed a good relationship with the human resources person who did the hiring.

Later in my career, as the manager of a larger operation, I noticed we were hiring and losing new employees at an alarming rate. We were experiencing 24 percent turnover at our lowest point. I brought this concern to a few of my supervisors, and they said the candidates were terrible. I asked them more questions of why they felt the candidates were terrible, and they explained the scenarios taking place. One supervisor, Fred, explained how his new hire said he did not know if he wanted to work with our company but would try it for a couple of days and "feel it out." Another supervisor, Jackie, said she had a new hire say he needed to go on vacation in one week but would only be gone for two weeks. The obvious problem with this situation is that the trainee will forget a lot of the training because he or she is not practicing and progressing what he or she learns each day. The more I started to think about our turnover problem and some of our turnover employees' comments, an idea came to mind. I called some of the new hires who left quickly and asked them if they would mind sharing a few thoughts about their hiring process and why they chose to leave. Some responded, while others never returned my call. The company had an exit interview form, which was supposed to be filled out (by us) whenever the employee quit or terminated and came to pick up their last check. I now became painfully aware of why this procedure was so necessary. If the previous manager and I followed this procedure, as the manager over this operation, we would not have had such an issue with turnover. I knew I must use this tool, which the company proved worked in the past and present. I not only used it but also started to find excellent results from the information I gathered.

The former employees who spoke to me shared things about their hiring process. Some of the accounts were a bit shocking and very eye opening. One former employee told me they were told they would be placed in one work area during the walk-through interview but were later assigned to a different area and job after they were hired. This was the fault of the operators, not the HR representative. Another employee explained that they asked to start a couple of weeks after returning from a vacation, but they were told it was okay to start now and still go on vacation after one week of training. This was not a good practice by the HR representative. Another employee told me the supervisor was too busy to train them, and the supervisor just walked away during the shift and never came back to finish training. In a successful business, a supervisor must communicate if they are unable to train a new employee. This allows the manager to shift trainers to where they are needed. *Training incorrectly is not an option.* Lastly, another person told me the job was too physical. I asked them if they remembered seeing the people working during their tour of the operation as a candidate. They said yes, but it did not look hard when they were watching. (We will talk about graduated workloads in chapter 5.) After hearing all these accounts from the former employees, I knew I needed to team up with my hiring representative. We needed to change a portion of our orientation during the hiring process.

When I met with my hiring supervisor, Rhonda, who worked in the human resources department, I asked her what she thought of the turnover problem. She started by saying it was not too bad for such an odd shift time for people to work, 4:00 a.m. to 9:00 a.m. This told me she did not see it as a problem, yet. After I explained how frustrated my supervisors were becoming with trying to train people who did not even really want the job or had to leave for vacation, she became aware that I investigated this issue already. Rhonda told me many of the supervisors had a bad attitude toward training new hires because they did not like to do it. I listened to her feelings and agreed with her that there were two supervisors, whom I was aware of, who did not like to train new employees. I explained I would carefully oversee any new hire in those supervisors' areas to prevent or reduce further turnover. I also offered to observe these supervisors to ensure that proper training was being performed.

I then asked Rhonda what she felt we could do to further reduce turnover. She first responded by saying that it should be reduced enough if I took care of those two supervisors. I informed her that only one out of eleven employees left from their referred work areas. I asked her whether we should hire employees who stated that they were going on a planned vacation *after* their first week of work, and then returned a week later. I asked her if any new hires had mentioned the idea of starting after they returned from vacation. She said they did, but she knew we needed help right away, so she asked them to start before they left. (This is important to note: Rhonda thought she was doing a good thing. She thought she was helping us out, and therefore, it was extremely important I did not admonish her or ridicule her effort.) I explained to Rhonda how I appreciated her effort in trying to hire good people to help us in the operation. Because I offered *empathy* toward her in order to solve this turnover problem, she was quick to open and told me her own issues—her long hours, the difficulty of her job, and that she was being stretched between two work areas. No one could perform a job efficiently under those circumstances.

Coaching Point: Do not stop a person who is venting with frustration or anger. They are telling you what they feel is holding them back or hurting the company.

Allow them to talk (although you may have to remind them of proper or acceptable language) and listen with empathy. Try to hear what they are saying, not how they are saying it. Let them know you care about what they have to say and that you are willing to listen. I found out very quickly, when I came out of college and joined the workforce, that most people who were upset about something in their job were upset because they cared. If they care, they will want to work with you or their manager to fix the issue. Do not take someone being upset as a bad attitude, necessarily. A football coach of mine (Steve Wichar) told me years ago, "If I don't yell or talk to you, then start to worry." He explained when he cared about a player, he wanted them to be successful. He watched them perform and knew when to compliment them and when to correct them. Although his care and passion for a player's success sometimes came out in yelling form, it did not mean he did not like the player; he simply wanted him to succeed by doing it the right way.

I could view all these comments from the supervisors and HR personnel as not being the company's, interviewers', supervisors', or my fault; but the truth was it was our entire fault. Nevertheless, mostly, it was my problem to solve.

I needed to get a handle on this turnover problem before I lost control of my operation. I was the leader. I had to develop a plan with my team, enact the plan, and lead us to achieve success. You may ask why having high turnover can cause a manager to lose control of their operation. Once an operation experiences turnover, it starts to become more difficult to hire and train. The attrition rate at which employees leave is naturally compounded by the number of employees who quit. Training needs soon outnumber trainers available to train. The new hire will leave due to negative reasons from lack of training. The turnover problem becomes like a snowball rolling downhill when you are continuously hiring to replace the person you just spent a week interviewing and training. It grows bigger and picks up speed, damaging things that get in its way. Once the supervisors cannot keep up with the amount of training required, for example, training two new employees at the same time in separate areas, they become frustrated. This costs time and money and inhibits production, service, and safety.

> The costliest factor to a company is employee attitude. (Thomas DePetro 1988)

Think about how the attitude of an experienced employee changes when they know that a new, less experienced person is coming in to work with them. They will have to work harder to pick up the slack of the new employee. I term this occurrence as a program because it does not happen over time, not in one moment and during group decision meetings. I will spend time discussing the effects of attitude on each portion of a company in another chapter.

Therefore, whom should you hire? You should hire the person who has a passion for the skill set of an available position and compassion for people. This person should be a good fit for the culture of the company. The person should fit well with those they will work with and the manager or supervisor they will report to. This person should be trainable, have a good attitude, and take pride in whatever they do. Lastly, this person should be caring. They must care about others and want to help others achieve success.

Hire me; I have an attitude.

This sounds like an oxymoron, but it is not. I have found that most people who become upset or frustrated at work is because they care. Think about something that does not upset you, whether it is a person, place, or thing. In most cases, you will realize you do not get upset because you do not feel strongly about whatever this something is. I have also realized that people who want both themselves and the company to be successful become agitated when things do not go properly. What comes off as a "bad attitude" may be because the person has a passion for what they do and what the company needs from everyone. They just need a leader to guide their energy in a more positive manner.

I recall a past supervisor (let us call her Jane) who was assigned to me for a large operation. I was informed by managers above me that Jane had the reputation of having a bad attitude. I was told I would probably fire Jane or want to trade her for another supervisor within the first two weeks of taking over the portion of the operation in which she worked. I told them, without meeting Jane, she would probably become my best supervisor knowing what I knew about "bad attitudes." This presumption became true, and the other managers even wanted to promote her and have her assigned to them within five months. How does this happen when these same people wanted to fire her just several months earlier? Three factors were accountable to this 180-degree change.

First, I listened to Jane. She worked in the operation several months before I even arrived. Jane went on a rant for about ten minutes, while I heard her out. I felt she was relieved that someone took the time to listen to her, and she was not going to waste this opportunity. Jane explained how every time she asked someone for help, which she needed to do her job, she would not get help. She would ask for tools, equipment, and a plan; but it never came. Again, I had to let Jane vent. She went off when I asked her to just tell me how she felt about the operation and her role. It was the first time anyone showed her how they genuinely cared about her and the operation. Once she calmed down, she told me all the issues preventing her from being successful. I told her I thought she was a caring person, and we would develop a successful plan together.

Second, her frustrations stemmed from a driver manager who would not give her a solid plan to begin the workday. Having no set plan, she still attempted to work and make her own adjustments. I asked her if she had approached the manager and explained how much she needed a set plan. She informed she asked several times but still never received an actual plan. I explained to Jane how we could approach this manager together and explain our needs. If he were unreceptive, we could then go to the next level. It turned out that he was not capable of making the plan but had to delegate this assignment to his supervisor. We found two problems in this equation, and I worked with the manager to resolve both.

Third, Jane was frustrated with not having enough supplies or tools that were required to do her job. I purchased those for her the next day, and she was incredibly happy. Fourth, her work partner, a fellow supervisor, was poor at training and holding people accountable. He wanted to be everyone's friend instead of a leader and teacher. I eventually had to replace him due to his inability to change, and the new supervisor I teamed up with Jane proved to be a much better fit. Together, they brought success within their respective area and the company. I mentored Jane and showed her how to use her energy in a more positive direction. She was promoted a year after I started to work with her, and I am still immensely proud of her to this day.

Eight months later, I had to tell the managers who wanted Jane to work for them that they couldn't have her. I jokingly told them we fired her eight months earlier—recall, this is what they wanted to do. They laughed, but my point was understood. Do not look to fire a person because of their bad attitude; seek to train and mentor them to be their best. Firing is only necessary if the person refuses to change, or in other words, firing is only necessary when the person does not care.

Remember, you need to seek the best available people to join your company; and when they are hired, they should exhibit a good or great attitude. If you hired them, they must have something going for them in the first place. You must train them properly, find out what their goals are within the company, and help them achieve their goals. If you do not do these things, you may lose a good employee who only sees that the company lacks leadership.

I am always amazed at how many supervisors or managers fail to sit down with each person under their responsibility and ask one question, "What motivates you?" Doesn't every company want a motivated workforce? The easiest way to make this happen is to make time for each employee; ask them this simple question. You will be amazed when you hear that money is not the main motivator 100 percent of the time. Yes, employees want and need to make money, but they are motivated for other reasons. Money is just a means to make ends meet, such as feeding their family. Why do some do more than they are asked to do? Why do some do less than they are asked to do? What prejudices cause this?

If an employee is talented but feels your company is doing nothing to train them in order to enhance their pay, promotions, or advancements, they will find another company to work at. You need to spot and attract the best available people, and then you must retain them. How will you know how to find the best people? By using the "principle of primacy," you will find ways to find the best people. This is discussed in the next chapter.

4

The First Thing Learned

Live as if you were to die tomorrow. Learn
as if you were to live forever.

—Gandhi

The "principle of primacy" states (paraphrased), "That which we learn first, we learn best and retain the longest." Under the rules of learning, "*primacy*, the state of being first, often creates a strong, almost unshakable, impression. Things learned first create a strong impression in the mind that is difficult to erase. For the instructor, this means what is taught must be right the first time. For the student, it means learning must be right" (Wikipedia.com).

Think about simple things you learned first: how to crawl, walk, talk, run, eat real food vs. baby food, drink from a cup without a lid, get up on a chair, get dressed, tie your shoes, ride a bike, open doors, say "please" and "thank you," look both ways before crossing the street, etc. How many of these have you forgotten how to do? Unless you were in an accident or another reason out of the norm, you still know how to do these things.

Then why is it that we learned early on not everything could be done alone, but we need someone to help us? Yet as we grow older, we think we can do everything ourselves. Why is it that when we were infants, we instinctively knew God would provide for us, but when we get older, we forget how God still provides for us? The reason I titled this book *More Than You* is because accomplishing things in life requires you, God, and the people in your life at certain times. According to the Bible, Moses asked God who he should say sent him to the pharaoh. God responded, "Tell him, I Am Who I Am." Therefore, God called Himself I Am. Some of us think we have total control of our life, and so we say or think that we are so great. As you can see, this is backward thinking. It's not our own doing that makes us great, but recognizing God's assistance in our efforts is what makes us successful.

When we were babies, we did not know we needed someone to help us. We were just aware when we were hungry, tired, and had an irritating diaper. We did not like when someone stuck their face an inch from our nose unless they were giving a quick kiss. (I am guessing this is the case, but why else do babies cry when people stick their faces so close to theirs and keep it there?) When we were hungry, we cried; and as a result, someone fed us. How did we know to cry? It was a God-known response. God taught us or gave us an instinct, and we trusted it, and guess what happened? It must have worked if you are alive to read this book. I say God knows exactly what we need.

When we were tired, how did we know to sleep? Remember, we were not intelligent enough to understand the doctor-recommended eight hours of sleep per day or any health benefits. New research just released in November 2016 shows that those who get more rest make more money. In fact, most babies sleep more than eight hours a day, and pediatricians agree it is needed in the infant stages for growth and development of the mind and body. Well, who taught us this? Again, I say God taught us to do it instinctively. We just trusted God, and it worked out for most of us. The same goes for crying when we had a wet diaper.

Therefore, the first principle of primacy is to trust God. We did it instinctively as a baby. Why is it then when we start to work on a business, we initially start with money matter or financing, a business plan, a business model, marketing needs, product acquirement or manufacturing, charters, or bylaws? Why don't we start with prayer? Why don't we go to God, or your higher being, and acknowledge that we are infants in this new world of business and that we need Him to teach us to know what to do or do what is Godly? Why does the principle of primacy make perfect sense in every other situation, except when it comes time to rely on God? We know we had to rely on Him as babies before we had thought and reason, and it worked. So why avoid it as adults?

I have done it myself. I think the only valid answer I can offer is when I thought I earned the position of opportunity, I had to continue to perform on my own. God performed through me. I forgot to live this and started to believe I, alone, was the reason for my success and failures. I put added pressure on those around me and on myself. It is a grand illusion (to borrow a phrase from the music group Styx), but one that is easy to believe. You will have supervisors, managers, or executives tell you what a good or great job you are doing. They will brag about you to others. If you want to eventually crash and burn, do what I did and start believing them. If you want to remain successful, give your credit to God and the people you work with and let the rest take care of itself. Remember, it is about more than you.

My first advice for getting into business straight out of college either by yourself or with another person is to pray. It was something you did before you could do anything else, and it worked. Do not stop it now if you "think" you can do it alone. Starting with God will allow you to make decisions, which will remind you to subconsciously ask yourself if God thinks this is a good idea. Do I love to perform this work? Is it ethical? Is it moral? Is it going to help people? Is it profitable? My guess for why so many people do not pray before starting a business or joining in on a business is because they think God doesn't want them to make money or prosper. Nothing could be further from the truth. If one takes a moment to read the Old and New Testaments, they will see God prospers those He calls, and they answer obediently. I will offer just a few examples, but trust me, there are many, many more, so I suggest you take the time to read the Testaments yourself. The knowledge and wisdom you will gain will be beyond your imagination. Here are a few verses to get you to validate my statement about God wanting you to prosper.

> God blessed them and said to them, "Be fruitful and increase in number; fill the earth and subdue it. Rule over the fish in the sea and the birds in the sky and over every living creature that moves on the ground." (Genesis 1:28 NIV)

Now, does not this sound like God wants you to prosper?

> "For I know the plans I have for you," declares the LORD, "plans to prosper you and not to harm you, plans to give you hope and a future." (Jeremiah 29–11 NIV)

I have this last one in a plaque on my dresser, and I remind the Lord every day how much He wants me to do good work and help others. I know how much He wants me to prosper. I just ask for His help.

I could offer many more quotes, but these are just two to get you started to understand that God has nothing against prosperity or money, but rather what we do with it. Just refuse to make money your god and remember it is a tool.

Now, if we know the principle of primacy is important and we know it is a fact, then how can we apply it to our job?

We want to start with praying about decisions we are going to make (wisdom) to ensure that we will not forget this is how our life started. It is what has cemented our success.

Next, we want to make sure we hire people who are passionate about their work. This was discussed in chapter 2; remember, hiring a passionate person is hiring someone who is using their principle of primacy because this passion is what God has placed on their heart. You are now working with God in making the new employee and your business what God wants, which is to prosper.

Now comes one of the most critical areas of running a successful business and the one task that never ends: *training*. We can find the best and hire the best, but if we do not train them properly, they will leave as a frustrated employee, and we will be left wondering what happened to the positive person we hired. The rule of primacy is critical in this discipline of training: that which we learn first, we learn best and retain the longest. We must start the employee out clearly, slowly, and properly for them to develop into the kind of excellent-performing employee we want to help run the company. The simple concept I want you to keep in mind is this: *speed comes with repetition, and repetition comes with time!*

We will discuss training in chapter 5, but I wanted to bring it up in this chapter regarding the principle of primacy. This principle is one of the facets of training that many people do not understand and, therefore, fail to follow when training new employees.

If you look at the table of contents, you will see that you can apply this important rule to every chapter. It will make a difference in whom you hire, how you train, how you communicate, how you hold people accountable, etc. It is a concept that will guide your thoughts and actions in creating a successful approach to how you tackle day-to-day challenges. This will eventually accumulate in your success. In addition, you will be perceived by your employees and investors as someone who understands the little important things, as well as the large grander things. You will be perceived as highly intelligent and capable.

5

Proper Communication

We have two ears and one mouth so that we
can listen twice as much as we speak.

—Epictetus

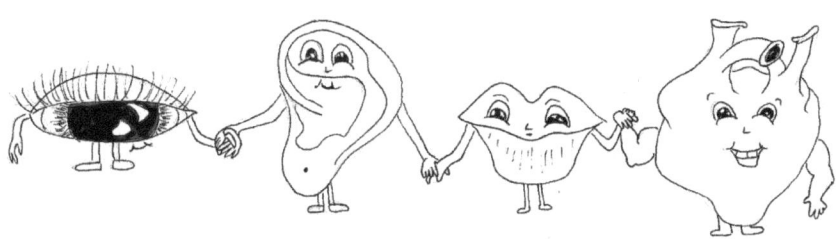

Have you heard the funny example of poor communication that involves the railroad spike holder and railroad spike pounder, or spike driver?

One man is holding a railroad spike in the location where he wants it to be driven into the ground. The other man is new to the company, and his job is to use a sixteen-pound sledgehammer to drive the spike into the ground. The man holding the spike says, "When I nod my head, you hit it."

It is okay to laugh at this point. I know I did when I first heard this joke.

This has always been one of my favorite examples of the challenges of communication. Both men thought they knew what they were supposed to do, and the message was so simple. How could this clear message be so misunderstood? The holder of the spike referred to the spike as "it," so when he said, "When I nod my head, you hit it," he meant for the spike pounder to hit the spike, not his head. The spike pounder was new and was probably nervous. He wanted to do whatever he was told to do and impress the boss. Out of nervousness, he thought he was supposed to hit the man's head since the command was "When I nod my head, you hit it." Thankfully, this is not a real-life story, but it is a great parity for how even an amazingly simple message can be extensively misunderstood.

Another reason it is one of my favorite jokes is it shows that a misunderstanding by the message deliverer, or the message receiver, can have devastating consequences to the person, job, and/or company. So in this scenario, who is at fault: the man stating the command or the man listening to the command? They are both at fault. Therefore, communication is vitally important.

One of the most common challenges for a company is proper communication. Communication is often lessened or absent from where it starts and where it ends. Those who know what they want to happen find it difficult to get the message to those who must make it happen.

The most important accomplishment of proper communication is how it solidifies the relationship we have with the other person. In order to become successful at anything, we must be successful at building meaningful and valued relationships with those closest to us, if not all people. Improper communication can lead to failure of a relationship, failure in carrying out a task, loss of trust in a person, feeling of failure as a person, money being lost, frustration, and loss of good employees. Successful communication can positively affect all these issues.

To prevent such failure, there are times when it is okay to say, "No, thank you, I don't think we work well together." This is what I had to tell someone once, and we never worked together again. This ended up being a loss for both of us. Let me explain the story in more detail to make this kind of situation clearer.

During the summer of 1982, I worked for a family friend (let us call him Fred) when I was a freshman in college. Fred worked as a public servant, so he used his off days from his job to make some extra money doing general labor jobs. He was a good and generous person. He gave to the community, church, friends, and friends of friends. However, his two bad qualities were that he was a lousy communicator, and he had a short temper. Looking back, his poor communication caused him so much anger.

Therefore, this one summer, I took a job with him painting houses. Fred offered me $800 per week. I was going to college, and in the early 1980s, this seemed like a lot of money. He asked me if I had ever painted before. I assured him I had. He asked if I had ever been up on a ladder before, and again, I assured him I had. He then went on to explain how we want to start painting the eaves of the house and work our way down to the bottom of the house. This made perfect sense to me. It was a systematic approach, top to bottom.

He then spent the next five minutes telling me how important it was that I did not miss a single spot on the house. He went on and on about making sure I painted under the bottom of the boards on the house. When anyone looked up, it was vital the board was covered properly in paint. He went on to describe how easy it is to miss a small spot, and if this happens, the spot will stand out like a sore thumb and make us look incompetent or unprofessional. He further explained how I needed to be careful not to put too much paint on my brush and to be sure not to allow any to fall on the ground. Too much paint on the brush could build up on the bottom lip of a board and look unprofessional. He had me so worried I would not paint right, so I took every precaution he told me. He left me to paint a certain side of the house, while he painted the other side. When he came to my side later, he found I was only done with a forty-foot area of the house at the same time he painted one whole side of a house. He asked me, in an angry voice, what I had been doing for the last thirty minutes. I explained how I was painting. He watched me and told me I was painting a house as if I was painting the Sistine

Chapel, and this was not how one paints a house. He was so upset, but I did not dare tell him I was following his orders to be careful. The two mistakes he made, as my employer and trainer, were his overemphasis on not making mistakes and not emphasizing to paint at a good pace. The second mistake he made was in how he trained me or rather that he clearly did not train me. He simply told me how to do the job. We will discuss training in the next chapter.

My mistake was that I did not clarify or repeat back to him how I should paint. I made an unknown mistake of not asking Fred how fast I should paint, so this was my fault. Based on what he told me, I thought it was all about quality, but the reality was that I needed to paint with quality and speed.

The point I want to make about communication is the person who is delivering the message must understand that just because they know exactly what they mean and they feel like the message was communicated properly does not mean the trainee understood it thoroughly. In my story, Fred assumed I knew I had to keep a good pace going. However, the reality was I did not know this was important. I thought doing the job with exceptional quality and ensuring that no errors were made were the most important aspects. I made this assumption based on how much time my employer spent emphasizing all the errors that can occur and to make sure I covered every inch of boards on the house. I thought this was his way of telling me to take my time and do it right.

In his mind, he made it clear to me that I should do the job well and quickly. I wish I could have read his mind because it would have saved both of us some frustration. Since we cannot read minds, proper communication is our best chance to accomplish success and avoid unnecessary frustration and stress. Most importantly, communication is key to enhance relationships with the people with whom we work.

As a quick lesson in painting a house and what Fred should have told me was to make sure I placed the paintbrush into the paint so only half of the bristles were covered in paint. He then should have said to tap the brush on top of the can where the bristles meet the frame of the brush. Tapping allows excess paint to fall off and eliminates the amount of paint dripping off the brush. Then paint the face of the board first by using most of the paint on the brush before using the little paint left on the brush to paint the underside of the board. Use long strokes with the brush when you first place the paint on the board. The brush will glide quickly and easily on the moisture of the paint. Then use smaller strokes to even the paint out if necessary.

I learned this when my friend and employer showed me how to properly paint a house board. It made perfect sense once I saw him do it. Imagine if Fred explained painting like this to me and then showed me. Do you think I would have worked at a faster pace? Would he and I have been more successful together? I could have completed the job in less time and with the same quality. Lastly, would I want to work with Fred in the future and make him more money in his side business? If only he focused more on proper training, perhaps we would have worked together again, and I may have gained more speed with time. I could have enjoyed his great sense of humor, which he had when he was not stressed at work.

Despite this mishap, we were on the same page with the painting projects. We both made money, and I appreciated the work. Fred said he appreciated having me as a crew member. A year later, he asked me to help him on a job painting inside of a home. He was doing some wallpaper work, but I had never done wallpaper work before. While I was painting, he asked me if I would stop and cut a piece of wallpaper to a certain length. I repeated twice the exact specification of the length he wanted me to cut. He assured me it was the length he needed, but to cut it a half inch longer if I wanted to, since he could trim the excess. I measured it out and added a half inch to the measurement. I brought him the piece of wallpaper. He placed it on the wall to measure to make sure I cut it properly. He exploded with anger when he saw it only reached the bottom of the wall in one area and was not long enough all the way across. He proceeded to call me every name in the book, including a few I had never heard of before. This, alone, was quite an accomplishment—given that I played on many sports teams and had heard coaches and players use some colorful language over the years. He brought the piece of wallpaper back to the cutting table and measured it himself. It measured what he told me to cut plus the half inch extra. What he forgot to tell me was the place he was placing it was on the stairway, and the bottom of the wall changes in length as the height of the stairs change. The top of the stairs may be fifty inches, but as the stairs go down, the wall space increases from fifty to sixty inches. Therefore, the paper needed to be cut on an angle to represent this longer area of the wall. This seems so simple to me now, but back then, I was new to this assignment.

So now I think it is clear why I told Fred, "No, thank you, I don't think we work well together." I did not stop working with him because he had a temper nor because of all the names he called me, although I didn't want them to become a permanent nickname. What caused me to stop working with him was when I realized he was a poor communicator and trainer. Therefore, the events of temper tantrums were not going to stop. Who wants to work in this environment every day? Therefore, I emphasize that the largest harm to a company, where the trainer of which does not understand how to communicate properly, is not the loss of money, product, service, or image, but the loss of an attitude.

Once a good or even great employee loses their good attitude, they will not work as hard or with quality. The person who loses a good attitude also loses a relationship. You did not hire a poor employee, and you didn't hire an employee with a bad attitude. You hired a good person who wants to make a living and help you create a good company. Your lack of proper communication and training will cause the loss of trust, appreciation, and desire to work. Their attitude will change, and their production and service will decrease. Now, you are left with an unhappy employee and an unhappy company. This is the sign of improper communication. This is where large cost is hidden in your company. Thus, communication is the biggest challenge in any company regardless of purpose, and it begins at the top.

I recall fishing with Fred one day on his boat, which took place after the painting job. He called me and said he was bringing a guest out fishing, and I might want to come along. The guest he brought was a man named Ed who had thirty-four years in management with ExxonMobil. Ed told me something on the boat this day that I will never forget and still use it to this day. Ed asked me what my major was in college. I replied it was marketing management. He explained he had over thirty-two years in corporate management and said, "One thing you need to know and remember is 98 percent of problems in a company are due to management." I respectfully questioned Ed on this idea and asked him about the responsibility of a union or the employees. Ed reminded me that a company is run by managers, not the union. The union exists and works within the company, so if there is no company, there is no union. The same principle is applied to employees. Therefore, the decisions managers make or agree to directly affect the success of the company. Ed smiled and said, "So you are getting into a career which is much more than management. You are going to be a leader." Leaders are responsible. I have reminded myself of this every time a discussion is brought up about who is responsible. If I am the manager (leader) of the area discussed, I tell the others that I am responsible. Even if my employee, supervisor, or manager makes a bad decision, it is my responsibility. I recall a comment that my district manager of a supply company I worked for made at a meeting to a group of managers. He said, "You can delegate authority, but you cannot delegate responsibility." How right is he?

Have I ever failed at communication? Yes—more than I want to recall because it still stings. When I realize that if I communicated better I could have enhanced my life and those of others around me, I wish I could go back and change how I communicated. One example of this was when I was a young supervisor and had some good ideas of how to make the operation better. My manager was a nice man; and he, like most of us, wanted to impress his boss and prove he could improve the operation. He was more of an engineer than an operator, but he was a good person. I would tell him my ideas, and he would always bring them up to his manager as an idea "he" came up with to make things better. I grew tired of this behavior since it made me feel betrayed by my manager. I grew resentment, and not only did I not share new ideas with him anymore, but I started looking for ways to speak poorly about him to other supervisors and his manager. I found other supervisors had the same feelings about this manager as I did. My desire to make him look more incompetent was successful. This coupled with his habit of staying in the office and not getting out with his workers caused his manager to remove him from his position. He was eventually moved out of the operation, and the company offered him a job a few hours away in a strange town. He had a wife and small child who had to move also. He did fine with his new assignment, but I wondered years later what could have been differently? You see, he was a nice person. He was intelligent in other areas of the company in which I was less knowledgeable. He had a good sense of humor and a desire to get along with people. I wonder if I had the courage to speak with him with honesty, if he would have changed his character defect and we might have become friends. Perhaps I could have learned how to be better at communication from him. I wonder if we could have been a strong team, which would have enhanced both of our careers. I wonder if I would have made a friend who would have taught me things about myself, which would have made me a better person.

Of course, I have made communication errors, and they usually damaged a relationship. Currently, I never stop working toward improving myself in this area. I know I have many opportunities to improve my communication, and my hope is that you realize this also. It does not matter if you are the giver or receiver of a message; you can enhance yourself, another person, and the company by proper communication. My wish is that you enjoy your work and avoid blaming others if things are not right or in your favor. Find ways to communicate kinder, more effectively, and in a caring manner.

My significant other, Holly, is an amazing person. She is so effective at looking at herself in any situation and asking what her part was if a poor result occurs. Notice I did not say "failure." I do not believe we fail at things, but instead, we find a longer road to success. We learn from everything we do or say, if we are wise. My Holly is incredibly wise, and she teaches me about myself every day. I listen when she evaluates a situation in her life, and she will ask what part she played in it. She has taught me to think this way with myself as well. This way of thinking prevents me from blaming someone else and looking into how I can communicate better.

When we disagree with someone else, sometimes the disagreement can become heated. If we both feel we are right or the other person did not hear us correctly, we can become passionate. One of the many things I love about Holly is how she will apologize, calm me down, and explain she just wants what is best for her or me in the matter, depending on which one needs to improve. She is a great communicator and always points the finger at herself. She has taught me to point the finger at myself. I have realized that things become better when I exhibit this kind of behavior.

One of the best ways to communicate properly is to ask the person with whom you are speaking questions about what they heard or what you stated. A good way to do this is to repeat what they said back to them, but in question form. If you are speaking to a person and you are delivering a message, keep it short. Explain both the message and the desired result clearly. Here is one example of delivering a message.

Imagine you are speaking with a coworker named Susan about enhancing customer service. You initiated the conversation: "Hi, Susan, I want to talk with you about ideas to reduce our customer complaints." Ask Susan to repeat back to you what you just said. You tell her, "The customer complaints are at 10 percent, and it is causing customers to lose trust in us, as a company." Again, ask Susan to repeat back what you just said. Voice your concern, "I'm concerned the customers will leave us." Once more, ask Susan to repeat back what you just said. Lastly, make sure she understands you thoroughly, "I want to make sure I'm communicating properly so you understand what I mean. I know you and I can team up for some great ideas on improving our customer satisfaction."

Susan will repeat back to you what she heard. This may or may not be the same thing as what you meant. When she tells you what she heard, it will tell you if your intended message was received correctly. If Susan's reply is different from what you attempted to say, explain to her how you did not communicate very well and would like to rephrase what you meant to say. This will allow her to feel better that she did not understand correctly and that it was not intentional. Your reexplanation will allow her to trust you. She will better understand that you are there to fix a problem, not ridicule her. It will allow you to communicate more effectively and continue to build a strong working relationship with her, as well as other coworkers.

As an example, let us say Susan replies, "You said I'm not doing a good job, and the customers are complaining more." This shows that Susan misunderstood what you said, and it allows you to rephrase your statement. You can reassure her that you did not say she was not doing her job well. You were just making a statement about the number of customer complaints, which could be due to a new product, service, or some other reason. You can assure her that you value her input and just want to understand her ideas on the matter. You can explain how she may have ideas or angles you have not thought of in your assessment. Therefore, it is so important to avoid making a statement and then moving on. When we need employees to become involved in the solution, and to do so, we must ask them to repeat what we said.

If she correctly repeats what you intended, you reply, "Great, we are on the same page. Can we share our ideas on what we think is causing the issue and suggest ways to eliminate these complaints?"

Success, money, growth, and becoming a great company are all predicated on relationships with people within the company. Relationships are predicated on proper communication, trust, and caring.

The previous example concerns the proper delivery of a message. What about when we are receiving a message? How can we communicate more effectively in this case to demonstrate we thoroughly understand the speaker?

First, listen closely. In order to do so, you must open your eyes, ears, feelings, mind, and heart to the message. If a distraction causes you to listen with less than 100 percent of your ability, ask for a quick moment to solve the issue, or disruption, and then proceed. Here is a real example of what I mean. I asked a neighbor of mine to come over and speak with me in the driveway whenever he had a spare moment. I informed him via e-mail that I wanted to ask his opinion on a subject. When he came over to talk, I asked his pardon and got up from my chair to turn off my radio, which was playing softly in the background. (You know what Bob Segar said, "Just take those ole records off the shelf… I'll sit and listen to 'em by myself.") I love listening to good music of all genres, but not when someone is speaking to me about an important matter. The music can become a distraction to my listening abilities.

When listening, use your eyes to understand the body language of the messenger. It will tell you if the person is happy, sad, urgent, angry, neutral, tired, or simply relaying a message. Sometimes someone might say something that is seemingly offensive. But if he or she is smiling, this might show that he or she meant for it to sound sincere. I will explain this in more detail in a moment.

As another example, I once interviewed for a wholesale distributor position. I was hoping to acquire a career in management, and I envisioned a position in training or operations. The interviewer was the head of the company's HR department. She asked me what brought me to their company and why I wanted to work with them. She asked me what experience I had in management and what job I felt I performed naturally. I remarked about my operations ability and achievements. I kept the comments 98 percent about operations experience and training ability and 2 percent about sales, labor, management, etc. When I was finished answering her questions, she stated, "I can tell you are passionate about sales." You may think I am joking, but I assure you I am not. You see, she was using her eyes and hearing my passion. She was projecting where she thought I would excel and used my comments about my previous success to allow herself to see me succeeding in her vision of sales for the company. I am confident in this field because I have had other hirers tell me I should be in sales. To briefly back others' belief in me—I was in the top 7 in the country for my company when I worked in pharmaceutical sales. The eyes are a powerful communicator.

In addition to using your eyes, use your ears and try to detect the tone of the person speaking. Is the person caring when they speak? Are they speaking quickly, showing they are in a hurry? Is the person trying to find the right word or words to use? A message can have many nuances, and our ears pick them up. I have come to be better at distinguishing between when someone *wants* to speak with me, when they *need* to speak with me, and when they *must* speak with me. These words (*want, need, must*) have different intensities and importance to the message, where the difference between *need* and *must* is that the latter has higher urgency. I have learned from listening to others use these words how I can better communicate by correctly using these three words for different situations. Ears are beautiful; is this why God gave us two? I have heard the saying that God gave us two ears and one mouth so we can listen twice as much as we speak. I think this is wise advice. I am trying to get better at this every day.

Use your mind when receiving a message. Remember, the other person has a boss. They are asked to do a job and do it successfully. Is there someone else with them as they approach you? If this person is their boss or coworker, understand they may speak in a slightly more business manner than they usually do. If the person approaching you is laughing and smiling with the person they are bringing toward you, they are more relaxed and may want to converse in a more lighthearted manner. The mind will also allow you to decipher whether this message is old, new, urgent, or nonchalant. You will better understand what question you may need to ask or what affirmation statement you need to give to the other person. The mind is a supercomputer if utilized correctly—it will allow you to recall, respond, or ask a question with accuracy. It will also remind us of a time or two when we responded appropriately, and things went well. It will help us to recall those times when things did not go so well and remind us how to avoid the same result.

Lastly, but perhaps most importantly, listen with your heart. I think caring is the starting block to much of what is good in us. When we care, we are able to accomplish great things and overcome many obstacles. I think listening with the heart is a way to say we will achieve a lot more success than just listening with our ears. The heart will tell us if the person delivering the message is just doing their job. It will tell us if the other person cares and if they need our help. It will help us to forgive someone if they deliver the message in the wrong tone, mindset, or manner.

The heart is like a brain surgeon. It cuts through the hard skull to get to what really matters.

When my kids became older and began saying hurtful things to each other or myself, I learned to listen with my heart and hear what they were really saying. Sometimes people say mean or wrong things, but we can see with our heart that they did so because their feelings were hurt. Other times, our heart will show us that the other person is happy, which explains why they were joking with or complimenting us. Our understanding comes from listening with the heart. The more we can understand a message, the more we hear its true meaning and not just the words. This is not easy; it takes time and practice.

Once we listen to the person communicating, it is important to repeat the same words that person used in question form, as mentioned before. This will allow the messenger to know if they need to adjust their message so you can understand it better. In addition, it will let the messenger know if you heard the message correctly or if you did not hear a part of the message that you needed to. The old saying that we cannot read minds is true so far. The only way to know if we heard the message correctly is to repeat it back to the messenger. If the messenger tells you that you are correct, then you can proceed with agreement. You can ask a question about a detail or explain that you do not understand. Here is an example dialogue of how to listen and restate a message:

> *Messenger*: John, I need you to go to the store today and pick up a cake.
> *John*: You want me to go to the store today and pick up a cake?
> *Messenger*: Yes, correct.
> *John*: Which store do you want me to go?
> *Messenger*: The ABC grocery store, one block away.
> *John*: Oh, the ABC grocery store one block away?

> *Messenger*: Yes, just go to the bakery and pick it up.
>
> *John*: Just go to the bakery and pick up a cake. A cake already made or order one with a new message behind the counter of the bakery?
>
> *Messenger*: I had a cake made for Susan for her birthday, and it is ready to be picked up at the bakery inside the counter area. It reads, "Happy Birthday, Susan."
>
> *John*: Okay, so I'm to pick up Susan's birthday cake, which is ready at the bakery inside the store. What name is on the order?
>
> *Messenger*: It's under my name.
>
> *John*: Okay, it's under your name. Do you want me to go right now or at lunch?
>
> *Messenger*: Yes, please go now. This way, we can all celebrate with Susan at lunch.
>
> *John*: Sure, I'll go now. Is it already paid for, or do I need to get some petty cash?
>
> *Messenger*: It's already paid. I paid for it when I ordered it.

This is a simple example to illustrate the process of good communication. Only by repeating the statement did John know if what he was hearing was correct. If John did not ask these questions, he would have not known if the messenger wanted John to go to a different store. He would not know there was a premade cake. He would not know when to pick up the cake. The best way to receive a message is to listen, repeat it back, and ask questions. The better we listen, the better we communicate. The more effectively we communicate, the better the results, and the stronger trust grows. The more trust we have in each other, the more successful a company and its people grow. I have always been number 1 in operations I have been assigned or have been asked to lead. Upper-level managers have asked me why I feel I'm successful. I tell them three reasons: (1) I care. (2) I communicate how much I care. I communicate proper training. Am I perfect at communication? No, but I am aware that I must work at becoming better every day. (3) I know who my good workers are, and I let them know I appreciate them. The people who do not want to help others, do their job, or get along, I encourage moving on through accountability.

I find it funny how almost everyone I have met in my life tells me I talk too much. When they see that my operations are number 1, they come and ask me why I am successful. I want to smile and give them a short quip, like "Who knows?" I laugh when they ask me more questions, meaning they want me to talk more, even though they also say I talk too much. However, I keep in mind something my mom used to remind me many times when I was frustrated with someone. She would say, "Everyone is at a different point on the path of life." This was Mom's way of saying some people have not learned this lesson yet.

In a more recent example, I experienced the pain of miscommunication with the owner of a construction company I worked in. He called and asked me how many people I had working this day, to which I responded, "Five people." He said, "Send them all home." I questioned him, "All of them?" This is when I learned his son was on the phone with us. He and his son said in unison, "Send them all home." I said, "Yes, sir." I knew this was not a good idea, but I was not going to argue with the man who started this company thirty years ago, so I sent the entire crew home that day. The next day I found out how costly his decision was to the company when only three people returned to work. One of them told me in front of the group that another worker, Kerry, would not be coming back; he quit. I asked why. I was told Kerry needed more hours and found another company to work for after I sent them home the day before. Unfortunately for me, Kerry was going to be one of my team leads (foremen); thus, I lost a good, hard worker, and the company lost a good potential leader. When I called the owner and told him the news, he asked me why Kerry quit. I explained it was due to me sending him home the day before and not getting enough hours. His next comment was "You shouldn't have sent him home." This made me feel like laughing and crying at the same time. After hearing my explanation, he told me I had to keep good people working. This is a funny thing—he hired me because he saw something in me; he met and interviewed me and knew of my success regardless of previous industries or positions. Instead, he wanted to ignore my proper communication when I asked, "All of them?" I wanted to laugh, because the day before, the owner was adamant that I should send "all" home even after I clarified/questioned "all." If he were not so upset or intense all the time and would have asked me if there was someone on the crew I felt I should keep on the clock, I would have recommended Kerry. He felt he was always right. This happened too frequently when he said one thing and then later retracted it. I recognized this detrimental pattern after working for him for several months. I did not want to argue the point and decrease our relationship, so I kept this issue to myself.

I wanted to cry out in pain because he did not communicate well, which cost the company and me a good employee. It was his responsibility to communicate with the proper verbiage. He needed to know, since I made it perfectly clear to him many times before this, that if he told me to do something, I was going to do it. The result of his miscommunication was the loss of a person I felt would be a good future leader for that company. I tried to verify his command the day before, but he was aggressively sure of himself, so instead, I did what he demanded. Is proper communication important? You had better believe it, and it is equally important to work at it daily.

One point I would like to make about written communication is that it is not comparable to face-to-face communication. However, if need be, I have found that speaking on the phone or via computer is the second-best method of two-way communication. If you do not have time and must write information to communicate, regardless of the purpose, an eight-and-a-half-by-eleven-inch piece of paper is sufficient to communicate. I suggest only using about 60 percent of the available space due to the attention span and urgency of most readers.

Often, when we are trying to send a written message to someone, they read it quickly, especially considering that everyone today is in a hurry. We cannot even go in a drive-through lane without someone behind us honking the horn to get us to move faster because the vehicle in front of us just moved four feet. If our computer takes twenty seconds to boot up, we get upset and anxious. We have been trained to expect everything quicker and faster compared to only ten years ago. In business, many people sit down at their work area and attempt to read all the important messages at one time. If we proceed to give them a message longer than one page, they will not read all of it or will skim the message for important points. I learned this as a supervisor.

One day in 1993, I observed my manager (I will call him Kyle) read his house mail, while simultaneously discussing my daily schedule with him. I noticed that he opened his mail and threw it away in the garbage without even reading it. From this, you might surmise that the company was small or that this manager worked at a lower level. This company was in the top 10 most admired in the world at the time and was the largest in its industry. I asked the manager why he did not read the mail before throwing it away, and he said he looks for two things: (1) the length of the document or number of pages and (2) if it is stamped second or third request.

I asked him, purely out of curiosity at this point, what he does when it reads second or third request. He stated that he viewed it as important at that point and would read it. I started laughing at his methodology, but it gave me great insight into how higher-level operators work. Years later, when I worked as a staff employee in health and safety compliance for the same company, I sent all my messages on one piece of paper. Operators never received long documents from me. I received the best results for the quarterly safety results for each operation by simply listing the following on one page:

1. The number of injuries specific to the operation
2. The most frequent injury
3. The highest cost injury
4. The name of the person(s) injured
5. The activity they were doing (pulling, pushing, walking, running, lifting, grasping, etc.)
6. The type of injury (strained muscle, broken bone, cut, fall, etc.)
7. The body part injured
8. The safety training method used to prevent reoccurrence

I had more than one operator call me at the HR office and tell me how much they enjoyed this one-page format. In fact, the best call I received was from David, an operations manager for thirty-two years. He told me the company should have done this from the beginning and how much information he got out of that one page compared to much more information spread over several pages. It was the 8.5" x 11", 60–70 percent full page that proved effective. I wanted to keep it short and to the point. This format quickly pointed to the issue and discussed how to fix it. The busiest managers, leaders, and owners will not read a long document. These people are referred to as drivers, or type A. They want the bottom line, so I give it to them. I have learned if they want to know more than what is on the page, they will call you.

How does a company communicate with hundreds of thousands of employees every day and get the same message to everyone? I can tell you one way that proved to work for UPS, whose success is not arguable. I use UPS as the example because they are an outstanding company that communicates well to their over-480,000 employees daily. The company uses a prework communication meeting each day, which is a three-minute talk from the management team to their specific work areas. The talk is designed to accomplish one of three things:

1. Inspire
2. Inform
3. Instruct

When I was trained in a workshop to use this communication format, I was timed. I was told I had to complete my talk between two minutes and forty-five seconds and three minutes and fifteen seconds. I was told to be prepared to give my talk every day in my operation and to have a visual aid. Lastly, I was instructed to complete each talk with a safety tip.

Folks, I told you successful companies are not successful by mistake. They have a vision for where they want to go, and they communicate this vision to everyone in the company. They communicate (talk and listen) with the employees, including management, daily. Communication is one of the biggest challenges for any company. If you emphasize proper communication and make it a daily routine, you will find that your work area and company will surpass your competition.

Training properly is communicating, and communicating is training properly. One cannot train without communicating. One cannot communicate without training. Remember, training and thus communication never stop.

Remember to use small words to communicate with clarity. I have heard people attempt to sound intelligent by communicating with others using complicated words or words not used by most people. Unless you are speaking to a group of people with their master's or doctorate degree, do not use big words. In fact, I would argue regardless of whom you are speaking with, use simple and straightforward words. Simple communication offers less chance for error. Here is an example of using complicated words (extracted from *One Year Devotions for Men* by Stuart Briscoe):

> Punished for his intransigence was equally correct. But Pharaoh's ongoing obduracy and his unrelenting antipathy necessitated ever increasing disasters until he finally yielded.

I would have worded the first sentence above this way instead: "Punished for his refusal to change his viewpoint was righteous or just." I would have worded the second sentence this way: "But Pharaoh's ongoing stubbornness and his unending hatred brought on more severe disasters until he finally gave in."

Can you see how much easier it is to understand my phrasing of the sentencing by using simple words? Using unfamiliar words will divert your audience and lose their attention. If your audience is your employees, you will fail to gain their effectiveness due to their lack of understanding of your message. Keep it simple or KISS (Keep It Simple, Sherlock). You may remember Sherlock Holmes broke his crime-solving problems down to the elementary stages. Then when he explained the solution back to Watson, he would say, "It's elementary, dear Watson." By keeping your communication at an elementary level when speaking to your employees or audience, you will greatly increase your chance for success.

6

The Art of Training

It's all to do with the training: you can do
a lot if you're properly trained.
—Elizabeth II, Queen of Great Britain

One day before a large meeting with a VIP group of managers, I spoke with the industrial engineering manager of the operation at that time (let us call him Rick). It was apparent that Rick was extremely nervous, as he chain-smoked cigarettes one after one, nervous because the highest-level manager in our state was attending this meeting. That manager brought his head of engineering, head of HR, and a few other staff members. I was also in industrial engineering at this time, and Rick asked me if I was nervous. I was too young to know to be nervous. I was only twenty-three years old. I assured him I was just there to learn from the managers who had more experience and knowledge in the operations of the company. The meeting was organized because the operation was ranked the least best in the region, which consisted of three states.

When the meeting began, the state's district manager started out with a statement and then a question. He said, "We are here to fix the least-best operation in our district. I have asked all of you to be here because you have been in the operation in the past or you are taking over the operation. Now, who has ideas of how to fix this operation?"

Success Note: Never be the first to speak up in a meeting unless you are asked a direct question.

During the meeting, one thing became clear to me. I sat quietly observing; Rick's nervousness got the best of him and was overbearing his good judgment. He kept defending himself to everyone who made a comment on what was wrong with the operation and how to fix the problem. Although I was only twenty-three years old, I knew from sports training throughout my life to never make excuses for not being successful. Finally, the district manager turned his eyes toward me and said, "Tom, you have been in the operations as an industrial engineering representative for several months. What do you think the problem is?"

Have you ever had to tell your mom or dad which sibling did something wrong when the sibling is staring right at you with that grimacing look that they will get you back if you snitch? I responded, "Well, George, from what I can see, attitude of the employees is the problem, and it stems from the fact training and accountability is nearly nonexistent." Rick attempted to speak but was only able to squeak out, "I trained them myself," before George put up his hand and stopped him in midsentence. George reminded Rick that he directed the question to me, not to him.

George asked me to explain, so I explained that I had asked the supervisors what the job methods were, and they did not know them.

I explained I had asked them what the safe work methods were, and they did not know them. I explained I had observed the operation daily and did not see much training happening at all. I spoke of how I trained employees myself; they stated, "No one ever showed me this." I explained why I did not believe we could hold any employees accountable if we didn't train them properly. George asked me what training properly meant to me. I explained the proper procedure of training:

"Trainer explains, employee explains back. Trainer demonstrates, employee demonstrates back. Trainer follows up, trainer retrains."

Only after this process can we hold an employee accountable. He asked me when training ends. I explained it never ends because we are human, and sometimes we are caught into bad habits and need to retrain to get out of them. He then asked me where I would start to improve the process. I explained that I would start where the process is initiated, which is the unloading of parcels. George had a slight smile on his face at this point. I was happy he was my highest-level boss and not Rick, who probably would have fired me after my comments based on the look on his face. George asked me one last question: if I had noticed all the "stacking of packages" on the belt portion of the operation. I agreed, so he asked me how I would fix this. I explained that it needed to be fixed at the back end, which he further questioned. I explained that when I ran a smaller operation in a past job, one that set a state record, I found auditing the inside of the trucks caused the loaders to stop stacking. George jokingly inquired, "You actually audited your loaders?" He made the joke because it was part of our job description as supervisors, but one that many workers made excuses for to avoid doing. The meeting concluded, and George winked at me as a sign that he liked my answers. Even though I felt the world lifted off my shoulders at this time, I now had to implement everything I said, and I did.

Remember, we discussed earlier one of the principles of learning: principle of primacy.

Training the right way, the first time, is one of the keys to success.

If I asked you, why must we train properly? Some of you might respond that it is the only way for others to know how to do their job. Others might answer that training ensures that the employee does the job "our way" vs. what they might have learned elsewhere in another company. Some may state that we train in order to provide the best customer service in the industry. Moreover, some might even say we train so the employee will work faster. The latter mindset views that the more productive the employee, the more profitable the company. All of these are good reasons, but they are only pieces of the pie, not the whole pie.

We train others the same way we would want to be trained in terms of how we are treated as a person.

Would you want to take over a job where others count on you and where you have poor or even no training at that job? Training is an investment in the future of a company. Do you want to make a good investment or a bad one?

This will allow us to achieve our ultimate success, which combines both a successful business and a successful person. How do you plan to train others in your company if the trainer is not properly taught how to train? How will you be successful if the employees do not know how to perform their job on both a small scale and macro scale? How will you establish a successful culture? How will your company grow?

The largest hidden cost caused by incorrect training is *loss of attitude*. A loss of attitude, which you will read throughout this book, is the costliest expense in a business.

You will know when you find an operation with poor training. You will find current employees working harder than others, decreased morale, negative work environment, higher turnover, increase in injuries/accidents, lower production, increased sick call-ins, lower service to customers, and loss of a good attitude culture in the company. From that point, whom will someone take over the company someday, or will the company go under?

However, proper training also allows us to achieve the other person's end success, which is to be successful and bring home a paycheck. It prepares employees properly to whatever opportunity they wish to accomplish within the company. If an employee is successful at their current level, they will be given a chance to advance. Donna Tisdale is a great example of this concept of employees being successful at their current position and given the opportunity to advance. Donna was a recent college grad in 1989. She graduated with an engineering degree and was very intelligent and skilled in her field. Donna was also a very personable and kind person and was looking to grow into a management position with UPS. She had to complete a three month daily driving route within the time guidelines in order to earn an opportunity to advance. Steven Thompson felt Donna was not where she needed to be one week into her training. Steven wisely assigned another trainer to Donna. She not only excelled at her driving challenge going forward, but worked her way into a Corporate Management position for UPS today. She is a wonderful and successful person, and the company is more successful with her. Bob Crouch is one of my favorite people and managers I have had the pleasure to know. He is an excellent manager and friend of mine and once told me something I'll never forget: "Nobody wakes up and wants to fail or have a bad day at their job. Most everyone wants to do well and be thought of well by his or her coworkers."

This fact is a solid starting point to begin a culture within your company. We can begin a culture where everyone looks out for each other. We can build a teamwork environment where no one is overworked, but everyone achieves more together than he or she can do individually.

Some have said the word *team* is an acronym. It stands for together everyone achieves more. This is a fact, which Jim Casey has also professed as the founder/owner of UPS. Coach Lombardi also professed this and demonstrated it by winning five championships with the Green Bay Packers within seven years, 1960–1967. The great pyramids of Egypt show us an example of what can last thousands of years when people work together. No, I do not believe in slavery of any kind—I am simply recognizing what happens when people work together.

One of my favorite quotes is from Coach Lou Holtz, a football coach of thirty-four years, who said, "If you help others get what they want, they will help you get what you want." Isn't this what we are accomplishing when we train?

The new employee wants to feel comfortable learning the new job. If it applies to you, remember how it felt being a new employee. I recall that I wanted to be liked. I wanted to be able to ask questions and have someone show me how to do the job right, even if it took several attempts to show me. I wanted to be brought into the group quickly so I did not feel like an outsider. I wanted to laugh on the job and work well together with the group or my manager. I wanted to go home at the end of the day or night and feel I did a good job. I did not want to hate going to work. I wanted to know my paycheck was going to be there every payday. I hoped to vacation with loved ones when the opportunities arose. I wanted the company to perform well so I had job security. Everyone should want these same things.

Proper training will propel a company forward. Poor training will cause stagnation to a company, and if it is left unchecked long enough, it will destroy it. Train well, and train daily. Remember, training never ends. A well-trained employee will help you get what you want. They will help your company become great and successful.

The first thing to consider when training others is to train in groups of two or more. Why is this important? You will find that if you train only one person, and this person quits, becomes sick, or receives another job offer during training, you will be void of any sort of "backup." Remember, you hire someone because they are on a job hunt, but this does not mean your company is their only target. Here is a simple rule:

Hire and train at least one more person than you need to fill open positions.

If you need four people, hire and train at least five. There is a good chance one or more will fail to become an employee. For instance, an employee may do well in an interview but fail to pass an attendance policy. They may have trouble getting to work on time, or they may struggle to fill the job requirements for the hired position. I highly suggest you train at least two or more people at a time. If they both show competency and appear to be potentially efficient employees, you can decide who is the best fit for your company. If one quits, you have not wasted all the time and effort to start the training process all over for a new prospective employee. Besides, competition brings out the best in people.

I have witnessed companies train two employees who both performed well and were both hired. One was designated the full-time employee, and the other became a fill-in for employees on vacation or a personal day off. Usually, by the end of the first or second month, the latter second person was hired full-time. I understand that companies do not have the budget to overstaff, but not staffing properly can cost the company more. If a company does not staff properly, it can cause a failure in service. If you fail a customer's need, will they come back? Will you have to refund them money for lack of service? Will this customer tell other customers how you failed to service them, which caused the problem? What about accidents caused from not having proper staffing?

How do companies cover understaffing? Most companies will ask the understaffed employees to pick up or cover the work area of another absent employee. Pushing employees, even good ones, too hard can lead to injuries. Was the employee worn down from the workload? What will happen if an employee attempts to work too quickly and makes a mistake, causing an injury? Could this extra effort lead to employee burnout? It is significant to note again that understaffing is much costlier than overstaffing. I like to say that companies cannot afford to let good people walk away. Interview and hire an additional person for a position so that you have two prospective employees instead of relying on just one. In the long term, you will not regret it. Besides, if you are hiring good people, can you have too many?

An experience dealing with this kind of situation was when I worked as an operations manager for a construction company. Repetitively, I attempted to nicely explain to the company owner why it was critical to hire one more person than we needed. I explained the competition aspect, and I expressed the fact that people often quit. I also needed more employees in order to grow from two divisions to three divisions. The owner kept reminding me it was too costly and that we needed to get more production from our current number of employees. He said we were not making enough money to hire an extra person. I tried to explain how new employees needed time to acquire speed and production. He did not want to listen to me, even though I only have twenty-five years of leadership experience. So I only hired two new employees but really needed three. If I hired three employees, I could have had three team-lead employees, where each leader could train a new employee for a week. This would have allowed me to train new employees to have them ready enough to take simple calls from customers.

Sure enough, one of my experienced employees quit one week later. He had a poor attendance record, and I held him accountable. He decided to leave instead of changing his attendance behavior. As luck would have it, a customer called me and needed two of my experienced crew to complete a project for them. One of the crew had to have a specific license by the DOT (Department of Transportation). This left me with only one new crew member to handle all customer calls. Of course, at the same time, one of our most significant customers called us needing a quick delivery. I had no choice but to have my one-week-trained employee deliver the product. My new employee did his best but left the product in the wrong area. This mistake caused the DOT to call the customer at nine thirty the same evening and demand them to send one of their own men out immediately to take care of the product that was left too close to the road. This customer called me the next day, clearly infuriated, and threatened to kick us off the project if this happened again. It was both a loss of revenue and a loss of reputation, which had me very concerned. I now had to deal with more pressure than I should have had to deal with and move my crew around to ensure this irate customer was not disappointed again. This caused less satisfaction with other customers, who were postponed a day or so due to veteran workers being removed from their project. Is overstaffing too costly? As it turned out, I was able to implement enough of what I do know that works (the topics in this book), keep everyone safe, grow the revenue by 234 percent, while reducing expenses 1.7 percent compared to the previous manager. This was based on the same period from the year before.

The second step is to tell the prospective employees that they *can* do the job. You might think this is a silly statement. One of the first things new employees want to know is that they can and will do their job well. We want to assure them that many people have come before them and learned the job; thus, they are capable too. Next, point out a quality or aspect this employee has that the others do not and explain how you *know* they will be able to learn the job also. This injection of confidence will allow them to relax and listen to you. It will place their mind at ease and help them perform better. New employees are nervous, so help them relax. Almost every musician, artist, athlete, teacher, public speaker, etc., will tell you people perform better when they are relaxed. Remember, relaxed does not mean sleeping or reclining; it means they are assured and not anxious.

The other facet of training, which will allow the trainer to train more effectively, is to develop a training area in the operation, facility, or street (if you are in sales). The trainer has already successfully performed their own training; thus, teach prospective employees more effectively. Other already-hired employees also understand the training process and know this is where the new hire starts their training. This reduces the need for the trainer to spend too much time learning the detailed specifics of all areas, which results in excellent training of the new hire. When the trainer is the expert, the trainee will listen and do what they are trained to do. A line that divides a trainer and an employee/worker—a trainer is there to instruct how to do a job properly but not to do the job. If a company wants a worker, then do not hire a trainer. If you do not hire a trainer, don't complain when the job is not done to your liking.

Lastly, the training area allows the proper amount and speed of work to be placed on the trainee. It will be an area of less volume and will demand the trainee to learn the fundamentals of the job. You can introduce more work and increase their production as they progress. This is called graduating the workload. As the employee becomes more skilled, you can add more work to their area.

I currently work for a company that does not believe in using a trainer being on-site. Instead, they believe the trainer should simultaneously do their respective job at a productive rate and train at the same time. I do not have the time or the desire to list all the things wrong with this approach. Just for starters, I will say our company turnover is excessively high at over 60 percent.

So what does high turnover mean? It means more confusion in the company. It means less service to the customer. It means lower productivity levels, which result in higher costs. It means more injuries or accidents, causing extreme cost increase in work comp insurance, employee burnout, and loss of employee morale, which is the costliest of all expenses. Remember, responsibility does not go away because someone decides not to do his or her job. The responsibility is passed onto someone else. If one person is continuously picking up the loose ends all the time, then the risk for burnout grows. Continuity in your workforce results in the same people doing the job well and providing better service to your customers. When you experience high turnover, it means you have brand-new employees providing service to your customers. Who knows how to better service your customers, a new employee or a veteran employee? Unless they were not trained well, a veteran employee will know the nuances of how to provide a customer with the expected service from the company.

I recently attended an association networking function. My goal was to meet and build a relationship with potential clients in my industry to acquire more business for us and provide them with great savings and service. One of the owners of an engineering company asked me if a certain employee was still employed with us. I assured him this person was still employed and was one of my team leads. The customer informed me that the former manager took this employee off his service area, so this customer went with another company. Our company lost thousands of dollars because of this decision. Now, this is an example of a voluntary absence of an employee to the customer. It is even worse when the customer finds out the employee who serviced them became injured. Now, you lose service and reputation.

Later in the chapter, other jobs that a trainer should be doing to advance the company when they are not hands-on training will be discussed.

The first thing we want to do when training new employees is explain to them where the exits are in case of an emergency. This is often overlooked and mentioned as an afterthought, if even mentioned at all. I recall the first time I heard this as the first topic of a course or workshop. I thought, *Wow, this person has their act together. This company has their priorities in the right order.*

Next, tell the employee what you are going to train them each day. This is simply known as "tell them what you are going to tell them." It may include the type of training that will be taught, whether it is via booklets, DVDs, hands-on activities, computer, etc. Ask them if they know how long the training will last. Then tell them how long it is going to last. This gives the person an idea of how long they will be at work. Have you ever been brought in on day one of a new job and not know how long you are going to be there? It's unprofessional and annoying. Tell them how easy or challenging it will be. *Ask first and then tell* them when they will get a break. Again, *ask first and then tell* them where the bathrooms are located. Are you doing any of these items currently? How is your training program going?

Why should we ask them before we tell them? First, they might already know, and if so, you can engage them in helping train the class. This makes a person feel good and effective, and it demonstrates that they are observant. Second, it prevents you from coming across like a monotone drone. Have you ever been in a training class where the instructor sounds like Ben Stein with a monotone voice? You are praying someone will put you out of your misery quickly. You hope someone will ask a question, or the trainer will tell you he or she is done. (Nothing against Ben Stein. I love Ben; he is intelligent and makes me laugh.)

If you must fill out paperwork or employees need to watch DVDs or videos, take care of this part of the training first. When this portion is completed, take the trainees toward the work area, but remind them on the way where the exits, bathrooms, break rooms, water fountains, etc., are located. This will help them feel more secure and part of the company, and it may remind them to ask to use the restroom so interruptions do not occur later. Trust me, people listen better and are much easier to train when they do not need to use the restroom during training. It allows them to focus on you and not on the all-important room. It will also reduce questions later. Professionalism has many benefits.

Show the employee(s) which door they should enter, how to walk to the clock-in area or work area if there is no clock-in, and where to place jackets, purses, lunch boxes, etc. Remind them, and yourself, how an employee in their work area will meet them the next day at the entrance door and walk them through the first routine in the morning. Some companies call this the buddy system. Introduce them to the employee who will assist them the following day at the first opportunity you have. This will create an environment or culture of teamwork and allow the current employee to feel respected by you and the company. It will help minimize nervousness, and it will help the new employee perceive you and the company as very professional. If this is one of their first mental notes, they will proceed to perform things correctly and professionally beginning on day one.

Remember: Great cultures are made; they do not just happen.

The leaders of any company will teach their employees (future and current) what, when, why, where, and how much will be needed to do the job. The details, which are put in place "from the start" or in primacy, will carry over.

Once an employee is brought to the work area, if the job allows, quickly introduce the new employee to the person who will meet them the next morning at the entrance door. Introduce them to each person you walk past in their new work area. Again, it helps the new person feel comfortable and learn a name or two. This also gives you the opportunity to show respect to your current employees and compliment them on something. If time allows, it may give you a chance to announce to the current employee you are passing which employee they will be assigned to for their buddy system. Some work areas allow this time, and others do not. If it is unsafe to introduce them to their future teammates, then explain this as a safety precaution before you enter the work area. Explain to the new hire not to attempt to shake hands, as it is a distraction and may create an accident.

You may wonder what the effect of the buddy system is on turnover. The short answer: it is an incredibly positive effect, or negative in the sense that it decreases turnover. A system like this can reduce turnover immensely and create a great culture for your company.

The first time I heard of a buddy system I was a sophomore in college at Northern Michigan University (NMU). The head football coach, Herb Grenke, addressed the team and explained how hard all the coaches work on the recruiting process. He explained how happy the coaches are when the freshmen show up to camp each year. He explained this gives them a mental snapshot of the future success of the team. The coach went on to explain how many freshmen players leave during the middle of the night within the first two weeks of training camp. (We used to practice three times a day, starting with breakfast at 6:30 a.m., ending with our last meeting of the day at 10:00 p.m., and lights had to be out by 11:00 p.m.). After we all stopped laughing, because we understood the temptation, the coach said he spoke with the team captains who all agreed on the buddy system.

The system assigned each freshman player room with a seasoned junior or senior player on the team. The older player was to help explain *and show* the new player how to get to the dorm room and walk them through the itinerary the first day of camp. Later in the evening, they explained the plan for the entire week. They were to walk with them to the cafeteria and practice. They answered questions and just talked to them as a close friend to build a relationship. The older buddy was to explain how the severe pain and soreness would go away. They would explain practices occur initially three times per day, then decrease to two per day and then to one per day. The older buddy was to introduce the new player to all teammates and make them feel welcome. The older buddy was to prevent anyone from teasing or intimidating the younger buddy. They were to remind the younger player that they would be fine and make the team, instilling them with confidence. They walked them to the locker room, equipment room, meeting rooms, film rooms, weight rooms, etc. He was to be a friend to them, reducing nervousness and anxiety. Yes, the buddy was to remind the freshman when he was inviting trouble by acting less than humble. The one last point the coach emphasized was that all older buddies and the entire team, in general, were to encourage this person.

I am not too sure of the exact number of turnovers we had this year with the incoming freshmen players, but I recall the coaches stating that the buddy system caused a 75 percent reduction in turnover, or lost freshman players, from prior years. The other positive effect was that we all felt closer as teammates at a quicker pace. We felt like we were more of a family that looked out for each other. This is what a buddy system can and will do for your company, if done right.

As an example, in an operation I took over as a manager, we employed a similar system since we experienced 24 percent turnover. We were able to drop turnover to 11 percent in five months by performing two interviews (instead of one) with each new employee and implementing the buddy system. It is safe to say I have seen this simple, yet effective system work.

After the new employee becomes acclimated to their work area and teammate as a part of their training, step back and ask them if they have any questions. How are you going to know if they have any questions if you do not ask them or give them the opportunity to ask a question? Answer their question yourself, right? No. Tell the new employee it is a good question and ask anyone in the group if they know the answer. This gives you a chance to see who might learn quickly or was listening more intently. Good listeners make good leaders. Again, you want to compliment the question and anyone who knows the answer. If need be, give the answer to them if no one knows it.

The next steps to training are as follows:

1. Trainer explains → Employee explains back.
2. Trainer demonstrates → Employee demonstrates.
3. Trainer follows up → Trainer retrains.

I will break each of these down because this is the right way to train, and it goes hand in hand with the principle of primacy. Only the best companies in the world train like this. If you have not seen it performed in your company, ask yourself where your company is ranked by *Forbes Magazine* each year.

The first step in training is to explain the process. This may be preceded by your observation of the employee if they are already in your company. Let us use a new employee for this example. It is especially important the person you are going to train has a chance to visualize what you are going to do and what they need to do. As you explain, also perform the job physically so they can both process it mentally and get a visual picture of how the job is done correctly. This will give most people a sense of relief. It also teaches the new employee the lingo or terms that the company uses. The more the employee hears such terms, the more they can use them and communicate properly and effectively.

Most of us learn what we know by seeing, which allows us to learn something faster and retain it longer. In the 1980s, Harvard University did a study on the learning habits of people and found that 94 percent of learning is visual, while the other 6 percent combines other senses like sound, touch, and smell.

Once we explain what, why, when, and where we are going to show a trainee how to do the job (and they explain it back), then we physically perform it ourselves. If this sounds familiar, you may have been trained in public speaking. In public speaking, you tell the audience what you are going to tell them, you tell them, and then you tell them what you told them. Here is a key point when demonstrating a job to a new employee(s): while you are performing the job as the trainer, you are verbalizing what you are doing while you are doing it. Below are a couple of examples of using this process:

Scenario 1: Training a Sales Rep

You say, "You will notice I didn't park in front of the window of the office that I have a meeting in." (You ask the trainee to repeat it back after each sentence.) Then you explain, "This will allow me to organize myself mentally and physically before walking into the office. I want to check myself in the mirror to ensure there is no food on my face or in my teeth, my nose is clear, and my hair is in place. The next thing I am going to do is make sure I have my binder with my business cards and notepaper, as well as a brochure I want to show the person. Now, I am going to step out of my car and open the back door where my suit coat is hanging up. I put on my suit coat and take a quick look in my window reflection to make sure my jacket looks professional on me, meaning the collar is not half up and half down, etc. I am going to make sure my name tag is on and straight. Now, I am taking in a few marketing items to leave behind like pens, mugs, etc. I am taking my binder with the items and placing a smile on my face. I'm mentally preparing to respond positively to what the receptionist or the office manager might tell me."

> *Scenario 2: Training a Supervisor*
>
> You say, "I'm going to train you, as a supervisor, how to evaluate one of your employees." (You ask the trainee to repeat back each sentence.) "The first thing we do is look at the data on the employee. We look at their production, service, and safety record. Look at their employee record to see if they have a birthday, company anniversary, or any significant information you can congratulate them on when you speak with them. Check their start date. This will tell you how many times they should have been trained and retrained and which trainer might have trained them. If they have been around several years, you can ask them what training style they liked best and why." You continue explaining the process. "Next, we are going to tell the employee why we are going to do an evaluation tomorrow on their work performance. It may be an annual evaluation, or it may be due to poor performance. It may simply be a training opportunity for the supervisor to learn the form. It is best to give the employee an advanced notice so they do not feel blindsided and defensive when you evaluate them. You can also give them a copy of the form you will use so they know exactly what you are looking for the next day. Unless you are going to audit them under suspicion for theft or other illegal activities, give them a notice. This will take away the employee's frustration and nervousness, and more importantly, it will build trust and show that you also want them to succeed."

Remember, your goal is to ensure that the employee is doing their job properly. If the employee cannot do the job properly or has established bad habits, giving them a day's notice is not going to turn them into a superstar. Their habits will show up eventually, usually sooner rather than later.

The day before I evaluate an employee, I want to review the form and ensure I understand what each line means and what each part of the evaluation is intending. Now, I am ready for tomorrow's evaluation with the employee.

Note: Some people may think it seems irregular or counterproductive to tell the employee about their evaluation and inform them of what you are looking for in their actions. I brought this point up the first time I was trained to do this with an employee. My manager reminded me that the reason behind an evaluation is to ensure the job is being done the right way. We want the employee to understand that we are on the same team, and we want them to be successful. We want the employees to trust us. He also pointed out how giving notice to a poor performer does not hurt. If they show you they "can" do the job properly, you now have evidence that they are capable. Now, accountability is acceptable. If you see the employee is not doing the job the right way, you can ask them why and find an underlying cause like hidden attitude, which can be fixed. If they show you they "cannot" do the job properly, you now know where to start retraining.

The bottom line is you want your company to be successful. For this to happen, you need the employees to perform their jobs well. When employees feel they are being trained by someone who cares, they respond much better than when they feel they are being trained by someone who is trying to get them in trouble or catch them doing their wrong. I have had many employees thank me for doing an evaluation on them. When you do it right, the employee knows you care and that you just want their success.

I recall a time when I was an operations supervisor. I was taken out of the number 1 operation in the state for the company and placed in the least-best operation. I was placed with a mini–task force of fellow supervisors to turn the operation around. There was a lot of attention by executives placed on this operation and the results, daily. The company was losing a lot of money, and its reputation for excellent service was declining due to this operation. Now, the company was investing a lot of money in all of us to turn it around into a service excellence and profitable operation.

I was given two work areas my first couple of months. These were, according to my manager's manager, the two worst parts of the operation. How did I get so lucky? After observing the supervisors who were working in these areas, I noticed they were acting like employees and not supervisors. They were trying to help employees do their work instead of doing their own supervising tasks, like training or auditing. I also noticed they were not following their respective job methods that the company had developed over many years. These methods were critical for performing each job successfully. My first thought was that I needed to train my supervisors, but not in front of the employees. Completing this training in front of the employees would take away the supervisor's authority and superiority. It would also embarrass them. This would not be right, and it was not what I intended. I did not want to embarrass anyone, as I do not like to be embarrassed. I did not want the employees to see me as their supervisor, but rather to see my supervisors as their supervisors.

The first thing I did with my new supervisors was to bring them into my office for a meeting. I asked them who could repeat the method for the job they were responsible for overseeing. It became clear to them, and me, that not one supervisor in the room knew "all" the methods. I asked them which method out of all of them was the most important, the one method that allowed the rest to be performed. Again, not one supervisor knew the answer. I told them I was going to ask for permission to train them each day. I would train them daily in a classroom, post-operation. I explained they would be paid for this one hour each day. I asked if there was a day that any of them could not attend due to school or family obligations. The goal was set. The only item left was to gain permission.

I approached my direct manager and gained permission to train my supervisors for one hour, on the clock, each day for ten days. Easy sell since the operation was the least best (worst) in three states. What did I do the night before the first class? I gave the methods form to each supervisor. I explained we were going to cover this in class with role plays for the next couple of days. I asked them to study it, write down questions, and be thoroughly ready for class. I encouraged them to look forward to becoming experts in their job.

I want to fast-forward this example in order to emphasize the importance of training. One week after I began training these supervisors, the work areas only marginally improved. My manager's manager approached me and asked why my training cost went up, which meant his training costs also went up. He wanted to know who gave me permission. I explained that my manager gave me permission, but more importantly, I explained that my supervisors did not know their job. He was not happy because the overall operation was still at the bottom of the rankings, and my areas were only showing minimal improvement.

Another week went by, and the big boss (my manager's manager) called all of us up to the break room as a management team. He was fuming. He was under a lot of pressure and demanded all of us to start doing the work of the employees until we get this thing turned around. He wanted my supervisors to do hourly work and for me to do their job as supervisor of the work area.

If you are ever in this situation, do not speak. Just listen and agree. It is like when your parent is upset about something. If you speak at this time, you will make it worse and get in more trouble.

Another week went by, and my work areas went from worst in the operation to number 2. There was a noticeable difference. My manager's manager approached me and told me how much better things looked and asked what I did. He said the other work areas were lagging my work areas in performance. (I wanted to tell him I ignored his demands because if I do not multiply my knowledge with my supervisors, we would suffer greatly, but I didn't do this.) I explained that I continued to train my supervisors until they fully understood their jobs, which included correctly training their employees. I told him that I followed up each day, while running their work areas, and observed each of them training their employee(s). I would compliment them in front of the employee on their training accuracy and then speak to them in private after the operation if they needed to improve something. My supervisors grew in knowledge and confidence, and the employees became more confident in their supervisors.

This created trust and better relationships in the work area. Everyone felt they were treated the same. The training they received was uniform, and everyone was held to the same standards.

This time around, the big boss told me I was doing a great job. He wanted me to bring this up in the meeting, which he was holding after completion of the operation. I answered the same question in the meeting and explained what kind of training we did in the classroom and on the job. The big boss told my manager he wanted me to train every supervisor in the operation the same way I did my own.

The point of emphasis, in case you missed it, is nothing will get better without sound training. You can fix a problem temporarily by doing the job yourself, but it will never be a long-term fix.

Doing the job yourself is a short-term solution to a long-term problem.

Only when training is completed and everyone is efficient at his or her job from the hourly to the supervisor will the company then begin to grow.

The other point is that *training is never completed*. You must train all the time—it must be ongoing. If you want your company to have the lowest cost and highest service and keep employees safe, training must be performed daily. I recommend you add one person to train each day on your daily planner; thus, if you train one person a day, you will have trained thirty employees in one month.

One may ask, "What if I have less than thirty employees?" This is not a problem. Most companies require performance, service, and safety as three elements of each job. You can break one employee's job down into several categories of those three elements of the job. Train one element a day in terms of its highest importance within their job. If you place service as your top priority, then train the employee on the aspects of doing their job with 100 percent service excellence. For a customer service rep or a service manager, service excellence requires the following:

- Reading reports to determine most improvement needed.
- Scheduling meetings with the customer needing the most help.
- Preparing material and questions for this customer.
- Notifying other departments, which may need to attend this meeting.
- Role-play meeting with a senior customer service rep or manager.

MORE THAN YOU

- Here are some things to perform when training an operation employee on safety:
- Observe.
- Explain to the employee your observations.
- Compliment the employee on good performance areas.
- Explain how you want them to perform in other areas.
- Have them explain back what areas they need to be safer.
- Demonstrate how to perform properly.
- Have the employee demonstrate back to you what you showed them.
- Follow up in several minutes and/or within the hour.
- Retrain or compliment the employee.

One day, a division manager told me that every single day, someone is training someone else.

His point was this: either the employee, supervisor, or manager was training you *not* to train them by giving you an attitude or you are going to train the employee, supervisor or manager and demand the right way to do the job. Either way, someone is always training someone else on what was going to happen. He was right on the mark.

In sales, there is a saying, "Telling is not selling." Thus, "telling" is not training. In other words, just because you verbally vomit on a prospect does not mean the prospect is going to buy it. One must ask questions and listen to the prospect in order to know what is most important to them. This gives a salesperson room to make the sale. It is the same in training. One must observe, ask questions, and learn what the issue is before one can train effectively. The company owner of my current job tells others and me what to do but never trains us. He tells but does not sell. He does not show. He does not ask me to repeat back what he said. He does not ask me to demonstrate. He just tells. Verbal vomit is abounding. This would be fine if he had someone training us, but no employee or supervisor has been taught how to train. Therefore, our company is struggling tremendously. The more we struggle, the less training occurs. It is a vicious cycle.

Showing is not training. Again, we need to explain first and then show. Next, have the employees explain and show back. This is the only way to know if the employee understands why you are training them and why or where they need to improve.

You will regress without follow-up. I have seen too many companies train and not follow up. They assume the employee will always do what they were trained to do all the time. Follow-up is critical in training to prevent bad habits and shortcuts when performing the job. The more successful a company's productivity, the more follow-up they perform. Training never ends. During your follow-up, you should observe for a bit of time to make sure the employee is doing all aspects of their job correctly. How do you recognize good people if you do not follow up?

Retraining is the result of follow-up. Retraining is one of the reasons why a trainer should not be asked to be a laborer. Trainers need time to follow up, observe, and retrain. It is only human nature to start taking shortcuts in work.

The training process is repeated here to emphasize its importance:

1. Trainer explains → Employee explains back.
2. Trainer demonstrates → Employee demonstrates.
3. Trainer follows up → Trainer retrains.

I promised you I would discuss "graduated workloads" back in chapter 2.

Have you ever started a workout routine in a gym and found you were sore the next few days? If you are like me, you hate this feeling. If the pain is great enough, it will cause you to skip the next workout or two. I love the old *Saturday Night Live* skits with Hans and Franz. They were dressed like weightlifters and had foreign accents. They were famous for saying, "We're going to pump…you up." However, there is nothing funny about pain and sore muscles, for real. The same goes for a new employee starting a new job. Whether they use their brain, which is a muscle, or their body and brain together, they need to be trained gradually, or else acute pain can ensue and deter them from their job. As mentioned previously, this idea of a slow, or gradual, start is referred to as a graduated workload.

A great place to start with a graduated workload is the number of hours the employee works their first couple of days. Let us say the average employee works eight hours per day. You would want to start the new employee out at two to three hours per day for two days or so. Then as they become accustomed to the job, increase their hours to four per day.

You may keep them at four hours per day for the rest of the week. The next week, start at four hours per day and then increase to six hours per day by Thursday. This graduating of the workload will allow the employee to learn at a more comfortable pace and feel better physically and mentally about the job. It will allow them to have a more positive attitude about the work they are being asked to do. No one wants to feel like a baby for whining or complaining about how sore he or she is or how tired his or her mind becomes in the new job. The graduated workload is another reason why you want to have one work area in the company where the new hires train. This is an area of easier work demand and can be taken over by a fellow employee when the new hire leaves. Again, I repeat that you want to train two people at a time. This will allow you to have one new employee working a half day, and when they leave, the second trainee works the other half. If one new employee quits or is not working out, it gives you a new employee to train without having to go through the process of hiring again. My current company does not do this, and unfortunately, our turnover at the corporate office is over 67 percent.

Another good habit or culture to establish in the graduated workload is to begin new hires on Thursday. This allows them to only work two days and then they are off for two days, assuming your company does not work on the weekends. They can also rest over the weekend and feel better by Monday morning. This prevents the new employee from getting too sore and overworked, which can cause them to want to quit quickly.

Lastly, graduate the workload. The amount of work a new employee performs should be increased after the new hire shows they can handle the increased workload. This is done incrementally until the work in a specific area is being performed at an optimal rate, as though a veteran employee was working. This is called graduated workload because the new hire graduates or accomplishes the current workload and is ready to move on.

Develop a training packet. This allows you to track the trainee for thirty days or longer, if needed. The top of each page of the packet should state which day of the evaluation process the employee is in. For example, the top of page 1 reads "Day 1." You can place what topics you want the employee to be trained this day. Place a line for the employee and supervisor to initial the topics that were covered and understood by the employee. This packet will document many items, including the following:

- Employee attendance
- The day the trainee is in the process
- Areas you would like to train each day
- Documents trainee needs to review and sign
- Safety methods
- Service policies and practices
- Production results
- The trainer who trained the trainee
- Pertinent information trainee needs to know in their first month on the job (evacuation plan, benefits enrollment, pay increase, etc.)

It will also serve as a reminder to the trainer of what areas they need to train the new employee daily. It is a nice way to make it necessary for the trainer to sit down with the new employee, review what they have trained, and answer questions the trainee might have, daily.

When I was a new supervisor, I remember following the training packet as if it was the gospel. It gave me an outline of what I needed to train the new hire and how much to do each day. I referred to it all the time for the first couple of employees I trained. After a while, I knew it like the back of my hand, and it became utilized as a double checklist to ensure I did not miss any area of training for the trainees.

The one result I really enjoyed about a training packet is that it forced me, willingly, to communicate with my new hire. It allowed me to know them better by going through the sign-off section and answering any questions they had. This allowed me to find out if they remembered what they learned. I liked how it would encourage the trainee to talk and share their thoughts about the job. They shared feelings about fellow employees, the company, how they felt physically, what their family said about their position or company, etc. It created a better relationship between the employee and me.

A training packet is to a trainer what a map or navigation system is to a traveler. It offers an organized approach for both the trainer and the trainee. I know I felt the company that trained me and documented it with a training packet came across as more professional and organized. My current company does not have this. Is it becoming more apparent why this company has 67 percent turnover?

A training packet is a great tool for a company to review and identify their better trainers. The company can look at turnover and notice if there are one or more specific trainers who are accountable. Let's face it, in today's litigious world, having documentation on how you trained a new employee can expel many lawsuits or false claims.

The training packet is also a great way to know the exact day the new employee began. Again, the company I am currently working for does not use a training packet. I have heard my manager ask an employee the date of their first day on the job. This is both unprofessional and unorganized, as this is something the manager should know or at least be able to find without asking the employee. It is so important to care enough about employees that you know their first day on the job and how they did during their first thirty days. How do you know when to graduate their workload? How do you know if they qualified for the job? How else do you reward them? How do you congratulate them on their anniversary date?

This format for training, if followed properly, will put your company ahead of most in your industry. Although training will demand your time daily, when exercised, your company will sustain consistency, growth, and excellence. You will develop a culture of teamwork and service. Your people will kindly correct all safety shortcuts on the spot. You will have few, if any, workers' compensation claims. You will keep costs down and services up. You will greatly reduce claims of discrimination since you are training everyone the same. The team will care about the company because they know the company cares about them. If you want the best people available to apply to work at your company, make training known to your employees and they will make it known to the public. You will reduce your turnover immensely compared to turnover rates of companies that follow improper training practices. Can you imagine the kind of talent you will attract and keep with daily training? This will give you a talent pool for your next leadership position.

As promised earlier in the chapter, I will list a few other responsibilities you will want your trainer to handle, which is why you don't want them to work as both an hourly employee and trainer. I have been trained in both systems, and they are a night-and-day difference in terms of the quality of training. Here is a list of possible responsibilities for your trainers:

- Follow up with the people they trained.
- Fill out the training packet.
- Retrain.
- Audit the operation, service, or safety.
- Teach classes for new employees.
- Travel to other operations to train.
- Write notes or talk to managers regarding their employees.
- Write notes of compliment to employees to take home to their loved ones.
- Attend seminars of the latest changes to company services or procedures.
- Professionally train by giving compliments, recertification, etc.
- Organize training materials with updated format, binders, DVDs, pictures, computer programs, etc.
- Spend time talking to the employees to increase morale.
- Spend time talking to human resources about their challenges or new information coming out soon for the company and employees.

My list is not meant to be all-inclusive but rather to give you an idea of other areas where your trainer can be more useful and help your company grow stronger. Using employees as trainers is okay when it's necessary, but it is not a good habit to develop. I am all in favor of employees training employees, once the initial training is completed and the "right" way to do the job has been learned. I think the employees who demonstrate that they care perform the job correctly *all the time*, not just when they feel like it. They are useful if they are okay with training others as well as follow-up training. However, there are too many times when I have seen some issues with employees training employees. Examples of such instances include the following:

- The trainer employee is not in the mood to train the trainee.
- The trainer employee is not good about filling out the training packet.
- The trainer employee is overwhelmed trying to do his or her own job and train simultaneously.
- The trainer employee takes liberties at teaching shortcuts, which are not safe cuts.
- The trainer employee is doing it only because they receive extra pay. In other words, their heart is not into helping others.
- The trainer employee does not know all the reasons why a method is required, but just does it because they were told. They cannot explain why it is important to do the job this way.
- The trainer is a friend of the supervisor, manager, or boss and was given the position but does not really enjoy it.
- The trainer employee does not understand the proper training techniques.
- The trainer is not satisfied with the small or no pay for training other employees.

I have found that I was best trained when the trainer was a true trainer and not a trainer employee. While I have been trained by other employees and learned to do whatever my job required, I had to learn later more about the job I didn't understand completely due to inadequate training.

7

Safety as a Personal Value

Safety is something that happens between your ears, not something you hold in your hands.

—Jeff Cooper

Whenever there is an emergency, *priorities* tend to change, while *personal values* stay the same. Think of eating breakfast as a priority. Think of getting dressed for work or school as a personal value. If you wake up late and must be out the door in five minutes to make it to work or school on time, are you going to eat breakfast? The priorities change, don't they? Are you going to get dressed or go to work naked or in your pajamas? See, personal values do not change.

Make safety a personal value, not your number 1 priority.

Make safety a personal value about who you are and not what you do. This applies to companies also. I cannot tell you how many companies I have seen with great slogans, such as "Our people are our greatest asset" and "Safety is our number 1 priority." When I have been inside said companies, the first thing tossed out the window when there is a service or production crisis is safety and people's well-being. If you want your employees to take their job and the company serious, make sure your personal value of safety is a value and not just a slogan.

Do you remember when you were a toddler and you had to learn to go downstairs? What was your first fear—your safety, right? What was your fear when you learned to ride a bike? Your safety was your fear. Can you recall the first time you learned to swim? You wanted to know that you would not drown. Safety is always our first concern.

Those who taught us to walk, ride a bike, swim, or any other challenge, we learned to trust. Once we trusted them and they helped us, we learned to like them. We like whom we trust. Numerous studies have been performed on physicians on why they do business and work with certain sales reps; the results overwhelmingly show that physicians only work with those they like and trust.

Again, we go back to the principle of primacy. It is apparent that those who care about our safety on the job, we learn to trust. Once we learn to trust them, we like them and want to help them. Employees are people you want to help make the company great and to help the other employees do their job. Remember, I discussed earlier the importance of creating a culture in your company. You also want the employees to both trust you and want to help you make the company great.

If you make safety the first area of training and your most often area of follow-up, the effects will be staggering. I have achieved safety as my number 1 goal in every operation I oversaw, and we ran number 1 in every operation. When employees realized I cared about them first, the production, service, and safety records became important to them. Safety goes back to our most basic need, and we want to be around and work for those who take care of this need.

I recall an executive manager of a Fortune 500 company who was responsible for an entire state. Above and behind his chair was a sign that read, "If you don't listen to me, why should I listen to you?" The same goes for training employees on how to work safely. If you do not train them, they will perceive that you do not care about their safety. If you do not care about your employees, why should they care about you? Why should they care about the company?

I learned that safety is a daily way of life while growing up with my dad, who was absolutely cherished by my seven siblings and me. We loved him, trusted him, and wanted to be around him all the time. We would do anything for him. He taught us to be safe in anything and everything we did. When we were learning to drive, he would explain the safety habits he used. If he were teaching us to shoot a gun, he would teach us the safety aspects first with an unloaded gun, progressing to a loaded gun. If we were shoveling snow, he would properly show us how to use mostly our legs and less our back so we would not get hurt. He was just a very caring and good person who wanted safety to be our first concern. Someone might argue he did so because he was our dad, and I do not argue with that—he had more love for us than he had for a stranger. However, I also witnessed him teach safety to my siblings' friends, my friends, strangers, and even his friends. He truly just cared about all people. I used my dad as an example in many stories I talked about safety training to other employees when I was a safety district supervisor in a large company. I told these students about how my dad lived safety. If my dad ever worked as a safety manager, which he never did, he would have been the best a company would have ever hired. It was who he was, not what he had to do.

Some people may question how safety is going to increase sales, reduce expenses, or allow a company to grow faster than the competition. Let us take a good financial look at the effects of safety. I was an accounting major during my first two years of college; so I understand the bean counting all CEOs, CFOs, and presidents of companies are concerned about. I as well have "counted the beans" as a business owner; thus, I understand firsthand that safety makes the biggest difference in finances.

Safety has several costs associated with it, which most people understand because their knowledge is at the fundamental level. Such costs due to ignorance of safety protocols include the following:

1. Physician or medical cost to mend the employee
2. Sometimes ambulance cost to transport the employee
3. Hiring another employee to take the injured employee's job
4. Training another employee to perform the job properly
5. Workers' comp cost to pay the employee while they heal
6. Cost to clean up the injury area of blood, broken equipment, etc.

I once saw an analysis that stated the initial costs of an injured employee are like an iceberg. The initial cost you see on the surface is only 10 percent of the true cost, while the other costs are hidden below the surface. So what are these hidden costs? They are as follows:

1. Lost production of a better-skilled employee doing the job
2. Lost service resulting from a slower employee
3. Training cost of a new employee
4. Increased cost of operation due to a supervisor having to watch the area closer, which prevents them from completing other tasks
5. Potential cost of a fill-in employee becoming injured due to lack of familiarity—another safety cost
6. Other employees slowing down to prevent being injured the same way their teammate was injured—equating to lost production
7. Other employees down the process becoming injured due to a new employee not performing the job properly: other employees may have to work harder and faster to complete the same task

8. Work comp reserves that the insurance company will demand next year due to the injury this year, which can be up to millions of dollars for a large company or a company with a poor safety record
9. No raises or lack of raises due to increased expenses
10. The loss of service or production caused an operations manager to have a heart attack or chest pain. (I put this one in there myself. I know how stressful operations can be.)
11. *The reduction of employee morale and motivation in the operation.* This may be the single largest cost to the company. Employees have approached me numerous times to share their empathy for an injured employee and said they were not going to work too fast to prevent a similar injury. Most of the time, the employee was not in my work area when injured, but my employees voiced disgust over the company's methods of pushing them too hard.

As an example, I will share a personal experience caused by following safety protocols and avoiding any injuries when I worked as a district safety supervisor. At work one day, the HR manager told me the insurance company had returned $750,000 to the company for a reduction in accidents and injuries in our state operations. He also went on to explain how workers' comp reserves are computed by insurance companies using a five-year trend. If a company can reduce injuries and accidents in one year, it factors into the reserve owed to the insurance company for five years. How is this for reducing your expenses? Remember, this was not an elimination of injuries and accidents, but a reduction.

Imagine if the company you lead made safety a personal value, and from such, you eliminated injuries or reduced them to 10 percent of the current number. It takes a lot of production to save $750,000, and it does not prevent a human being from being injured. The operation I oversaw for one year was able to reduce the cost per package from $0.93 to $0.89. When you reduce injuries, it will result in increased morale, service, production, and employee satisfaction;

and the profits will follow. The funny part of this fact is how it also changed both my manager and the company.

My division manager complained to me how we dropped from 98 percent effective productivity to 90 percent. I informed him that we were training the newer employees to work at the same rate as veteran employees. We had just built a new processing building for the company and needed veteran employees to test the new building capabilities. The operation I oversaw had many new employees. He wanted to know why I was not as upset as he was. I showed him page 2 of the operation report. It revealed that my cost per piece was down from $0.93 to $0.89 per package. He did not know what to say. He asked if anyone from the district office called me on this. I told him no, but I am making the company money with safety leading the way.

My division manager came back to me two days later and told me the district manager was going to make the cost per piece his major factor in the success of the state's operations, ahead of productivity. You see, productivity only measures planned hours against actual hours. Cost per piece is the overall cost of the operation each day divided by the number of packages processed. It represents the true cost or savings of the operation. I did not initially know this would be the effect of placing *safety* as the top value. I just knew placing employees' safety ahead of all else was the right thing to do. Safety as a personal value still stands as one of the greatest values my dad taught me. This lesson has helped me at work and in my personal activities.

However, the best fact from all of this is that all people left the company each day safely and returned to their loved ones in good health.

When safety is a personal value and used as a principle of primacy during training, it results in a more productive, service-guaranteed, and profitable company every time. I know that this has been proven in my experience, as witnessed by the good attitudes of my coworkers and employees.

There are two solid methods to increase profits: reduce expenses and increase sales. (I do not mention increasing your prices because this gives your competition an upper hand.) Placing the safety of your employees above all else will not only reduce expenses, allowing you to keep prices of products or service low and outduel your competition by gaining more market share, but will make your company one of the most sought-after companies to work for by the best employees. Future leaders will flock to your company, and you will find the next best leader to continue the growth of your company.

All the methods to complete a task or job within any company should be based on *safety*, *service*, and *production*. I want everyone who reads this to understand an especially important point: you don't lose production or increase costs by working safely; you increase production and service while reducing costs. Anyone who thinks they will outshine their peers or industry by pushing employees and cutting corners in safety is heading for a major fall. I encourage every company to resist promoting people into leadership positions until they have first viewed their safety numbers. If an employee has a poor safety record in areas under their responsibility, do not promote them until they turn the trend around, period. If you care about people and the company, you will not allow them to become injured.

I hope this helps you understand why safety is number 1. It is not number 1 because we want it to be, but because it must be. Make safety your company's personal value.

8

Become a "1 Percenter"

If a man does not keep pace with his companions,
perhaps it is because he hears a different drummer.
—Henry David Thoreau

Be a 1 percenter. Think like a 1 percenter. Now, you might ponder how you might do this. Let me start with a personal example and then offer advice on becoming a 1 percenter. One day at lunch, I ran into an acquaintance, Mike, whom I used to wait on when I worked at a convenience store. Mike asked if I still worked at the same company since he had not seen me in a while, and I assured him I still did but at a different location. Mike also told me he golfed with the owner of the company I worked at and that he would pass on any messages I wanted him to relay. I made sure not to share any messages during my first year as I do not believe newer employees should voice too much of their opinions during their first year with a company. This is a general statement, and not all companies practice this behavior, yet I have found this to be true in all the companies I have worked at. In certain industries, such as computer programming, I have heard that Google, Yahoo, and Microsoft, among others, encourage suggestions and change.

    I explained to Mike that I was working at another location than the one we originally met, which was my third location within the company. Mike asked me how things were going, and I explained how the company has a decent customer service culture. However, I went on to explain the company could be so much better. I wanted to see improvements in communication and training in order to take the company to the next level. Mike asked me what ideas I had for these areas. I explained how I was sure the owner knew how he wanted his business to run, but I felt his methods were not carried out effectively. I felt this was mostly due to the lack of training from the people who train the managers.

    I presented Mike with a quick scenario of when I took over a poorly ran operation for a different company. The first thing I did was ask my supervisors what the methods were for the job. I then asked them to tell me the production, service, and safety methods, which they could not inform or explain to me. After revealing this, I asked Mike, "How are the employees going to do their job if the supervisors don't train them correctly?"

    I then explained to him how the company has a five-point greeting it wants every customer service person to communicate with each customer. I explained how it was not being carried out. I reminded him that the employees were not being held accountable, but even more disturbing was they did not understand how important this was to the company, the customer, and themselves.

    I informed him that not enough people were available to train at the same time. At the time, the three managers I worked for said that they requested more employees, but the company brought in only one new hire, who flunked out of orientation. Why would you bring in one employee when at least two were needed? I pointed out how this caused improper staffing issues and unnecessary overtime expenses within operations.

I explained to Mike the six points to training people properly (you have read this in chapter 5) and that this procedure was not even close to being followed in our company. I told him I was concerned and did not want to see the company fail or stagnate due to such practices. He suggested I write an e-mail and explain my concern. I pondered the decision before I finally requested a meeting. Did I realize it was "political suicide" within the company? Yes, I did. I did it because I am not afraid to fail. If someone does not like me for making the company better, then do not like me. The real question for people who do not care about the company is "What is your motivation for not wanting to make the company better?"

Mike told me at this point of the conversation that I was a "1 percenter." He explained 1 percenters care about the job, company, customers, and employees. He stated how many people just want to do their job and go home. According to Mike, employees do not want to improve or change anything but just want to clock in, do their job, and go home. I agree that many people do not want to think too much about the company or the job. This is not necessarily a bad thing, however. If everyone wanted to be a supervisor or manager, there would be no employees to do the work.

In addition, asking certain individuals to lead as a manager would cause the person discomfort and anxiety. It is okay that some people want to work as employees and not in a management or leadership position. However, I believe employees will be much better emotionally and mentally *if* they understand how their actions affect the growth of the company, the customer, and their future.

I am sure most employees do not understand how their incorrect actions could result in them losing their job, vacation time, pay raise, etc. Let us take the simple example of a customer service employee at my current company. Their responsibilities are to greet customers at the counter and complete a transaction with a five-point conversation. If the employee does not perform this every time, it could cause a customer to become frustrated, feel unhelped, and not feel a connection or loyalty to the store. This could result in loss of a customer or customers. Research shows that unhappy customers will discuss their dissatisfaction with a company to seven other people. Today, due to social media, this audience can extend to hundreds or tens of thousands of people. This may also cause the customer to become loyal to a competitor store in the area. If this scenario is repeated enough, the store could lose profits, and the owner could lay off employees or close the operation. The employee would now have to look for another job and lose their two, three, or four weeks of vacation time, decreasing motivation to even work at all. Do you think a new employer is going to offer the same vacation time or higher pay as the last employer where the said employee worked for several years?

We all want to know we have a purpose in life. I believe many of us want to know how we positively affect others and the world itself. I do not believe everyone wants to be an overachiever, but I do believe most people are good-natured and want to accomplish good things. A starting point is needed to allow people to care more and understand that they are important to others. My second point to explain is an acronym: What's in It for Me (WIIFM). Once people understand how they can help others and help themselves in the process, the rest is downhill. While some may argue that a company is not a person, I argue that a company is made up of people and each person is individually important in a company's success. From this view, each person can also attain the success level he or she desires.

Therefore, what is a 1 percenter? Here is my opinion:

A 1 percenter is a person who wholesomely "cares" for the benefit of others, a company or business, and themselves.

What things do they care for? They care about many things, but mostly they care about doing the right thing. If they work in a process that can be improved upon, they will share their ideas of how to make the procedure more effective, efficient, safer, less costly, and better for the customer and employees. If you can help the customer or employees at the correct cost–benefit ratio, you help the company.

MORE THAN YOU

I believe the reason a 1 percenter looks to do the right thing is because they understand how it positively affects others. In 1989, I worked in R&D for a company that investigated the future and desired to change parts of its operations from manual labor to automated equipment. Many of us tested equipment in order to find the best option for the company. Since I was brought into the process after the equipment was mostly in place, my job was to tweak the process or equipment. I was asked by my manager, Steven, who was the person in charge of the entire R&D project, to observe the equipment, particularly how the freight would react within such equipment. He asked me to take one or two days and do nothing but to just watch and think of a better way to complete the process. After watching for one day, I had a great idea, which I saw as a gift from God—a "lightbulb moment." Can you imagine if I observed this process for two days and came back with nothing? Steven's boss was on the board of directors of this mega company, so I was very thankful God opened my eyes and mind to this idea after one day.

I explained to Steven that changing the slope of the belt would eliminate the need for extensive roller systems. The freight could slide to one side of the belt if the belt was metal rather than nylon and if the belt was sloped. The roller systems were necessary due to the wide path from which the freight approached the roller system. This new belt could greatly reduce the need for such a long and wide roller system, thus reducing cost and materials for the company. An additional benefit is that it would prevent straps from being caught in the roller system, which caused jams and package breakage. My manager told me he liked the idea and asked me to put it in writing and give him a printed copy, while keeping a copy on my disc.

I was thinking of how this improvement would save the company a lot of money. I realized there were hundreds of thousands of people and families who counted on this company for their living. The stronger the company, the more stable the future was for these families. All of us who worked in management also held stock in the company, so I knew the more we saved, the better our stock would grow. Did I want my stock to grow? Sure, I did. However, it was the idea the company would have fewer expenses and have more money to pay us employees, reinvest in future ventures, and continue to grow that motivated me most to make sure my idea was successful. I personally received no bonus or compensation, other than my shares of company stock, whereby the stock might have a higher value due to the cost being lowered to automate the process.

A special person who is willing to help and do the right thing, even when it may cost them hardship or promotion, should be valued and not feared—a 1 percenter. Unfortunately, if this person is not allowed to improve the company or is stifled, they will often leave a company to search for another one that will work with them. Steven understood this point very well. He created an environment where his employees could be creative and share ideas. He saw the individual talent in each employee and encouraged him or her to use that talent. He challenged us to open our mind to bigger ideas and always complimented us for both effort and results.

I recently interviewed for a position with two midsized companies. One manager, an operations director, did not want to hire me due to his desire for me to stay under his area of responsibility. He asked me, "How long before you get bored and want to leave the operations manager position?" I smiled, looked at the human resources manager then the director, and responded I didn't think I would become bored since I wanted to operate a "showpiece" operation. This would require a little time to establish a vision, carry out training activities, develop a culture, and prepare an operation that he would be proud to call his. I explained *if* the time came after a few years when I became bored, my skills would allow me to work where the company needed me. I might be able to assist the company in various areas, such as training, or perhaps work in another division of the company like fleet fuel deliveries. The HR woman in the room thought my answer was exceptionally good and said, "Oh, that's a good answer. It shows you're flexible." However, the director became red faced and ended the interview within twenty seconds. He stated that the other positions I mentioned were not available in his area of the company. He told me that three to four other candidates were prospective for the manager-in-training position, and they would be trained to run a store operation. He stood up, thanked me for coming, and opened the door for me to leave. I knew I was not getting that job. Oops. I guess he cared less about how my skill set could help grow his company and cared more about his personal betterment.

In the second company, I interviewed with another manager who was the head of human resources. She asked me what I saw myself doing for the company. As learned from my last interview and not wishing to make her face red, I asked what area of the company my skills could be used best. She said she felt like I had a passion for sales, so I smiled and asked about a sales position. She also informed me of the swing trainer position in which I could use my skills as a trainer and assist with sales. I smiled large and explained how I would enjoy this position since it mirrored my skill level and desire. Then I asked her what kind of employees her company or she liked to hire. Did they want a person who wanted to stay at the position they were hired to perform or someone who wanted to grow with the company and move upward? She smiled and assured me that she and the company attempted to hire people who wanted to move up and contribute to the company's growth. I sincerely thanked her. Do you want to guess which company will have more success in the long term? I know my answer.

9

Follow Up and Never Stop Communicating

Either you follow up or you fold up.
—Bernard Kelvin Clive

Dances with Wolves is one of my favorite movies for many reasons. One of those reasons is that it shows how human behavior changes when left untrained. I reflect on the way in which Kevin Costner's character behaves when he is not followed up with from his commanding officer or fellow soldiers. He starts to forget his duty. He starts to write a lot in his journal. He starts to allow his mind to wander to the point that he befriends a wolf. (Costner is an incredible actor.)

One of the reasons he forgets his role as a soldier is because he was not followed up with enough and retrained. As it turns out in the movie, this leads to the betterment of his life. I also admire that the ways of the Native American Lakota were depicted in a beautiful and admiring form. I personally wish we had many of their customs in our current society. They were mostly a respectful people. They were conservationists, spiritual, wise, excellent teachers, intelligent, understanding, patient, and helpful. Tribe elders understood the importance of following up and retraining the youth if necessary. Men taught men, and women taught women trades. Men and women worked together respectfully and helped each other. They learned, taught, and grew as a community.

According to the laws of learning (Wikipedia.com), "The principle of *recency* states that things most recently learned are best remembered. Conversely, the further a student is removed, timewise, from a new fact or understanding, the more difficult it is to remember. For example, it is easy to recall a new telephone number dialed a few minutes ago, but it is usually impossible to recall a new number dialed last week. The closer the training or learning time is to the time of actual need to apply the training, the more apt the learner will be to perform successfully."

This principle explains the importance of constant follow-up. The employee is going to remember how to be successful when they are followed up with and retrained, if necessary, the proper way. The employee must be reminded and retrained on a continuous basis.

Too many managers and leaders feel that because they have trained someone once, the person is good to go. Be fair to yourself and to the employee. Regardless of what level they are in, follow up and compliment them for doing the job correctly or retrain patiently if needed.

My current company employed a twenty-two-year man in one division of the company—we will call him Jim (not his real name). He was knowledgeable of the methods and procedures required to complete daily tasks in his division of work. I invited him to my operation, with the owner's blessing, to train my people. He did this job much longer than I had and knew all the nuances. I asked him upon his arrival if anyone trained him how to most effectively train others, to which he responded, "Not really." I asked him if he knew the six steps to training. He said no. I reviewed them with him and explained the reason behind each one. He complimented me for sharing this knowledge with him. He said he had never heard this process before but liked it a lot. He said he was going to instill and follow these steps when training others. This made me smile.

The PAP (Positive, Accountable, Positive) is a process I named myself. The method is one I have found most people appreciate, especially if an employee develops a bad habit or forgets a method of their job.

Following this method, begin your review with what the employee is doing well—proclaim how their work is *positive*. Remind them of how you need them to do the other method correctly and why, and if they do not, you will have to take the next step—hold them *accountable*. End the conversation on an encouraging note—again, tell them their work is *positive*. Remember, when an employee knows you want their success, they will receive the training with open arms.

An example dialogue between a trainer and trainee incorporating PAP is described as follows:

Step 1: Positive

Trainer, Supervisor, or Manager: I noticed you are always on time for work and give solid effort. I appreciate how you take pride in your effort. You work safely and productively. Why do you do these things?

Step 2: Accountable

Trainer, Supervisor, or Manager: Do you recall how I showed you to make sure the product is installed correctly with attention to the quality look? I need you to perform the product install like this each time. I noticed lately you have been working quickly, but not focusing on the quality. Do you need me to retrain you? Okay, then you will do the installs the way I trained you? Okay, so you understand that if I see your quality is still less than I trained you in the next thirty days, I will have to issue a warning letter?

> *Step 3: Positive*
>
> Trainer, Supervisor, or Manager: I know you are a good employee, and you care about your job. I have no doubt you will install the product correctly from now on. Keep up the solid effort and working safely. I appreciate you as an employee.

I have used this method of working with my employees on accountability for years. I have never had an employee tell me they did not like how I held them accountable when I followed this format. In fact, most of the time, the employee would ask me if I noticed how much their work improved lately, if I had not already told them.

Another reason to follow up with employee performance is recognition. I always ask employers, employees, managers, and supervisors how you can properly hold someone accountable without following up to see how they are doing.

Accountability precedes recognition and reward. Follow-up is one of the steps of accountability.

When we see a person doing a job properly, the way they were trained, we could yell, shout, and jump up and down as a sign of recognition of the employee. We could celebrate a good job by an employee the way a football player celebrates a touchdown. We can do a happy dance, slam our clipboard down, high-five them, shake their hand, point at them, and give them the number 1 index finger. Remember to use the proper finger. I am making this point of excitement over the top with hopes you will take great joy when your employee does well. I hope you express your true feelings of how happy you are because of their performance.

Remember to take a few seconds to reward yourself with a compliment for your training. You cared enough to train employees the right way and to follow up. Now, celebrate before moving on. All work and no play makes us a dull boy or girl. Smile at yourself for the accomplishment. Thank God and give Him a high five.

Your follow-up will communicate several things to the employee. It will tell them the job they perform is important. It will show them that training is ongoing in your company and never ends. It informs them that you want to reward them but need the right reason to do so. It will tell them you will be back again. Most importantly, it will show them you care! How is this employee's family going to feel when they explain to their family how you complimented them, high-fived them, slammed your clipboard down, did an end-zone dance, and asked them to join in? Why would you not want this? Life is about more than you. You may have to request they do not call security on you, but this really shows how proud you are of them. This level of contentment is all possible by follow-up and ensuring the consistency of good work.

10

Goals

Setting goals is the first step in turning the invisible into the visible.
—Tony Robbins

The best and easiest way to accomplish your goal is to make it clear and specific. The following describes examples of accomplishable goals:

- "I want to own, manage, and lead a successful company to be the most ridiculously incredible service company to an extent that motivates others to write stories and movies about it."

- "I want to be the best writer and produce the most-read books in the United States. I want my books to help millions of people better their lives."
- "I want to grow a business and train my people so well that one of my employees buys the business and grows it bigger than I did."
- "I want to sit on my wooden reclined chair on the beach in Key West, Florida, drink my umbrella drink, and sleep in the chair all night. Repeat until rested. Set new goal."

Hey, who said you could not have fun setting goals? I have seen a pendulum swing in mission statements and goals for companies over the past one hundred years. No, I have not lived one hundred years, although my kids might argue that; but I have read examples of companies' goals over that time frame.

In the early 1900s, companies had simple goals. A farmer wanted to sell his crops to feed his family, pay off his land, and pass on his farm to his children. A storeowner wanted to sell goods to his townspeople to make enough money to pay off his home, pay for his inventory, and have enough to retire one day. Then when corporations were developed, we started to talk about service, production, and returning investment to the shareowners. The mission statement changed from one mission to several. The goals became multiple instead of one. Today, I think it is wise that many companies are going back to the basics in terms of their goals and mission statements.

Here are a few powerful mission statements from well-known companies that you may be familiar with:

- Pepsi—"Beat Coke."
- Honda—"We will crush, squash, and slaughter Yamaha."
- Nike—"Crush Reebok."

These goals are clear, specific, and easy to understand. A goal leads one to prepare steps to accomplish that goal. The great thing about goals is how they keep a company focused on reviewing the steps to ensure the result or goal is accomplished. An executive manager or leader can and should ask, "Will this step allow us to achieve our goal?"

The benefit of keeping just one simple goal is that this allows the rest of the goals to fall into place. When a company wants to be rated number 1 in service for their industry, the return to shareholders will be there when it is accomplished. The company will focus on training their employees well. If a company wants to be number 1 in quality for their industry, the growth in sales will follow, and the company brand will grow in popularity. The key to accomplishing such goals is to ensure that the expenses do not outweigh the available revenue. This is referred to as the cost–benefit ratio. If the ratio is high, the company will go out of business before it can realize its dream or goal.

This brings us full circle back to the principle of primacy: praying, hiring the right people, communicating, understanding personal value and safety, training properly, keeping the goal at the forefront, and following up to ensure things are moving in the right direction. Always keep track of expenses vs. revenue. You should be constantly looking for great leaders who will push and pull the company forward to success. They will encourage others to strive for greatness. They will create and encourage employees to think creatively. Leaders will make it fun to work and will make you think of things you have never imagined and realize it can happen. One of my favorite quotes is said by Chrysler's CEO Lee Iacocca in a commercial: "Lead, follow, or get out of the way." People like to work with good people. I like to learn, and if we are going to learn, why not learn from the best?

Lastly, I want you to remember a great quote by Johann Wolfgang von Goethe:

> What you get by achieving your goals is not as important as what you become by achieving your goals.

11

Accountability

Accountability breeds response-ability.
—Steven Covey

When I was eight years old, I gained permission from my parents to ride my bike three miles from our home to my childhood best friend Ronald "Jamesy" Specker's home. When I arrived at Jamesy's house, his mom told me he was playing in a baseball game at the fields. I rode a block to the fields to find Jamesy and watched him play with his little league team. After a bit, I realized Jamesy was not going to bat for a while, and I found myself browsing around the field when I noticed three kids playing ball tag. One kid would chase the other two kids with a soccer-sized rubber ball, and if he hit one of them with the ball, that "hit" kid became the chaser with the ball. The other two ran away to escape being hit. However, while watching them play, I noticed something scary. Several times, I saw one of the kids run between parked cars into the two-way street to avoid being hit with the ball. I wondered what would happen if a car was driving by. Would the boy see the car and stop? Would the car see the boy in time and stop? Several more minutes went past as I watched the game. I looked over to check on how those three boys were doing. At that moment, I saw the youngest boy run between two parked cars on the street curb and into the street. This time, a car was going by at about 25–30 mph. I could only get out the word *hey* and didn't get a chance to finish saying, "Look out!" The boy ran straight in front of the car, and the driver locked up his brakes as quick as he could. It was too late, the car slammed into the boy, and I watched him fly like a rag doll and hit the road about twenty feet from where he was hit. He rolled up like a puppet on the road. He didn't move. The driver slammed his car in park and ran to the boy lying in the street. This was in the early 1970s, so no cell phone was available to use. An adult ran to a nearby house and called 911. The ambulance and police officer came quickly and rushed the boy away to a hospital. A couple of days later, I found out that the boy was fine when I saw him walk by my house. I ran out to ask him how he was feeling to which he responded he was sore, but nothing was broken. I guess youth has its privileges. I believe he owes his guardian angels a solid for that one.

How many times can you recall your parent telling you to always look both ways before crossing a street? This constant reminder is called training. Accountability is what happens when training is not followed, which leads to retraining. Retraining is concluded when an employee demonstrates that they are mentally and physically capable of performing a job correctly. Accountability should not be thought of as something bad, but as a good method to prevent accidents, such as the car accident with the boy.

Discipline is bad for an employee who decides not to perform a task they demonstrated they could complete. What result do you think the boy in the above story would prefer? Getting restricted to the house for twenty minutes for not practicing what he was taught and not looking both ways *or* being hit and knocked unconscious by a 4,000+ lb. car moving at 25 mph? I will take accountability, thank you.

Here is an example of a positive accountability story. When I was eleven years old and in the sixth grade, I was walking home from middle school and heard a couple of my friends yell out to me. I walked over to talk with them and see what they were doing. They were each smoking a cigarette that one of the boys stole from his dad's car. They were my friends, so I did not judge them. I just talked and laughed for a little while and then finished my walk home. When I walked into my house, my parents were in the kitchen. I said hi and asked what they were doing. My mom said she smelled smoke. My mom never smoked, and she can smell smoke like a bloodhound smells a rabbit track. I told her how a couple of friends I ran into on the walk home were smoking, and the smell probably came from their smoke. I knew my mom and dad had told me not to smoke when I was younger, and they trained me on the side effects of smoking. Mom then asked me if I smoked, and I laughed and told her I was an athlete. It was already hard enough to run sprints and catch my breath without smoking. She said, "Good kid, your dad and I are going to take you for some ice cream." I realized looking back on this situation that an accurate reward and recognition (getting ice cream) could not take place without accountability. This case shows that accountability is a good thing—I shared with my parents that I was around people smoking when I could have easily lied. This kind of behavior should be sought by all. In a work environment, the only way to recognize a good job is by following up and using accountability to see what the employee is doing or has already performed. My mom said that if I did smoke that one day, I would have had to stay home and do dishes while she and my dad went for ice cream without me. I think she was joking, maybe not.

Accountability is nothing more than your supervisor or manager recognizing or retraining you to do the job the way you were trained in the first place. If you were not trained properly, true accountability cannot exist. Most importantly, true recognition for a good or great job cannot exist without accountability.

Now, there are exceptions to this rule. You may not have been trained to walk into work with clothes on, but it is common sense you would do this anyway. There are simple courtesies that we must perform in terms of common sense and knowing what is right and wrong. We know such courtesies exist regardless of whether we had taught them or not. For instance, we know not to urinate or defecate in the work area. We cannot hit another employee because we are mad at them or do not like them, and we cannot arrive at work late often.

Accountability is simply your manager or supervisor following up to ensure you are performing the job the best way possible for your own and others' safety, the best customer service, and in the most productive way. Typically, a job method has all three of these goals built into the process. Keeping you safe is not something we should dislike. While providing the best customer service seems to be best for the customer, it is also best for the employee. The customer is what brings in revenue, from which the employee is paid: no customer, no paycheck. Production is a company's way to prevent expenses from surpassing revenue or income. When production is low, payroll expenses increase, and the company loses money. This limits the growth of the company. If this can continue for long enough, it will force the company to go out of business.

Many companies will attempt to offset the increase in expenses by increasing the prices of their product. The higher the cost, the fewer products sold. Ask anyone if they would rather pay $20,000 or $15,000 for the same car. Ask them if they would rather pay $400 or $200 for the same TV. A company's continuous production equates to job security for the employees. I would imagine an employee would rather remain with a company for ten, twenty, or thirty years than switch companies every five or ten years due to a company "going under." The longer an employee stays with a company, the more increases they receive in vacation days, pay, benefits, and pension. Any employee who states they do not care about their company's production or service completely lacks an understanding of business and job security. Likewise, any company that does not reward a good employee in some form lacks a complete understanding of business and company security. As my mom used to say, "It takes two to tango."

Accountability is necessary for a company to perform and stay in business. Accountability starts at the top, where the leaders of a company must be held accountable. While this top is often assigned to a board of directors or CEO, the top of a company is held accountable by the customers. The leaders must hold those assigned to them accountable.

Why is accountability necessary? Coach Vince Lombardi said it best: "Fatigue makes cowards of us all." When we become tired, we start to cut corners. This leads to poor behavior, which leads to poor performance. As humans, it is in our nature to eventually grow tired of something, whether it is another person, a job, or an activity. Therefore, it is helpful and necessary to have someone remind us why we need to do the right thing or continue even when we are tired. This assists us in keeping focused. This is accountability.

Quick joke: Remember, when you get tired a second time, you are re-tired.

I never have enjoyed telling an employee they need to perform better, regardless of whether it was production, safety, service, sales, paperwork, or any other measurable field. I learned early in my career while still attending college that it is easier and more enjoyable to recognize good performance and inspire people than it is to hold people accountable for poor performance. I found that when I gave recognition to an employee for their good performance, at least one other employee would ask me to come by their work area to see how well they performed. This acknowledgment was usually due to me rewarding the first employee with food, giving a gift card, or even doing their work for them for several minutes so they could take break. This sort of reward inspired others to follow. Success breeds success.

In addition, I found when I recognized different employees for different reasons based on performance standards, it made the specific skills of each employee apparent. It created a real team atmosphere, caused fellow employees to compliment their peers, and often served as a motivation to improve in their respective areas.

One day, when I was a new supervisor, I recognized that a loader on the dock, Bruce, was assisting a fellow loader, Brian, on the belt. Later in the shift, I noticed Brian tell the employees working on the belt that he was going to "pull a Bruce" and help Steve, another loader. It became a joke, but it had a positive effect on those working on the belt. Soon, everyone was helping each other because they realized it made everyone's job easier. If one employee is hit with a lot of work while a fellow employee is not, combined teamwork creates a more efficient atmosphere and lessens the load on all who reciprocate. The employees will start to realize they may not get as many slack periods, but they will also not get overwhelmed either so that everyone has time to talk and work together. This comradery creates a feel-good environment, where each employee can feel good about himself or herself. If one person helps their peers, it is highly likely they will receive help back.

The WIIFM method (defined on page 53) means that the employee will always have help when work becomes difficult or fast-paced. The same employee will feel good when they help a peer. In addition, they will also find that they laugh more at the occasional, crazy work pace because they have a friend who is helping them, and they are both moving urgently. They are both in the same situation together, which makes it more fun to work, builds bonds and relationships, and develops a culture of success. The supervisor is also happy since there are fewer mistakes, employees are working together, and the work is being done safely. Everyone wins from teamwork.

Accountability forces a manager or leader to evaluate their employees. The leader becomes more analytical and discovers certain details that allow the leader to honestly recognize a good-performing employee. Another positive fact about accountability is that it avoids feelings of favoritism or discrimination.

Let us take a simple example of employees waiting on customers. Picture the following scenario: A manager looks at the printout of receipts and finds that one employee serviced 500 customers, while another employee on the same shift serviced 380. The manager compliments the employee the next day in front of the other employees to make them feel appreciated. The other (who serviced 380 customers) employee approaches the manager and explains that the other duties he or she performs prevents him or her from servicing more customers, while the other employee (500) does not have the same additional duties. The manager analyzes this information and finds out the employee completes these other tasks in less time than they are allotted. The next day, the manager recognizes the employee, not for servicing a high number of customers, but for completing a greater number of tasks in the minimal time they are given. This kind of recognition is based on accountability and analyzing data, or simply observing the employee and his or her responsibilities. This praise creates a positive work environment where other employees appreciate the teammate for their own set of skills. None of this happens without accountability.

Training without accountability is like shooting at a target in a dark room. Accountability allows a trainer, manager, supervisor, or leader to see where any immediate need exists or where more attention is required. Observing workers or analyzing data related to a job helps the trainer evaluate where to begin training and with whom. The resulting information may also help the trainer discover if there is a legitimate reason why the results are less than desirable for a certain employee. If there is a problem, the trainer can help provide solutions so the employee can perform adequately. However, the issue may simply be that the employee is not doing their job. In this case, the trainer holds this employee accountable and determines where follow-up training is needed. In another case, the problem may stem due to job safety or heavy workflow. This would alert the trainer to work with the operations manager to change the operation to make it safer or lighten the workload. A trainer may also find that an employee has developed bad habits, which would require retraining. The problem could also be caused by not having the right tools to do the job properly. An employee may have developed an attitude from something within work or outside of work, causing them to slow down on the job. The problem could be a substance abuse issue or family problems. As can be seen, there are many reasons and variables existing in the workplace that can result in a job not being done properly. Accountability is the starting point to discover the stem of problems and only helps to lead an employee to success.

What if an employee does not want to work anymore or has an attitude? Most employees want to work and avoid discipline. If a trainer investigates an issue, follows up to see if retraining is needed, and completes the retraining (meaning the employee can demonstrate the proper job), but nothing gets fixed, then it comes down to documenting. The trainer needs to ask the employee to stay after work or come in early the next day to review their write-up. The trainer will review the employee's record to learn how the employee was retrained and by whom and what the employee will be held accountable for to perform better going forward. Remember to use the PAP method.

The employee document should be dated with the time reviewed and should be witnessed by another person. If there is a union in the workplace, the union steward should be made aware of every step of the retraining process from discovery of the problem. When or if it comes down to discipline, the union steward should already be aware of the issue and the retraining and be present while the employee initials the form. Most employees will work within the guidelines of their job. Therefore, writing up an underperforming employee will be the exception and not the rule. It will become even less of an issue with other employees when they observe the trainer was caring, capable, and knowledgeable and held the employee accountable. I have had many employees approach me and thank me for holding another employee accountable. They would explain how much more work they or another employee had to complete to cover for the employee who was not doing their job.

If an employee chooses not to work as instructed, the employee will receive the next step in the disciplinary process. If the behavior is still not corrected, the employee will be further disciplined, or their employment could even be terminated. Many companies will follow a four-part process to discipline, which includes the following:

1. Verbal warning
2. Written warning
3. Time off without pay
4. Termination

Any of these steps can be used back-to-back before progressing to the next step, based on time and circumstances. Most employees will improve before termination is necessary. If there is no improvement after given numerous changes, remember, you did not fire the employee; they fired themselves.

I am 100 percent against any employee being held accountable by a trainer when the employee or the trainer cannot complete the job as designed.

When I worked as a medical home health representative for a company, I initially applied to the sales manager position, but they wanted me to prove myself first. Ten months later, I was held accountable by a new trainer in sales who worked with me for two hours of an eight-hour day. She could not get into two offices I called on. I asked the receptionist, whom I previously had a great rapport with, to allow us to see the physician. The receptionist stated she would do it as a favor to me, but she did not like the way my trainer approached her. The trainer did not acquire any closed sales or business for the company on this day. To make matters worse, she told me that my territory was too large. She also scoffed when I told her I was a sales rep in the industry for ten months. She, the trainer, stated it takes eighteen to twenty-four months to establish trust with offices and referral sources. Yet she called me the next day and told me she needed to have a sit-down review with my manager and me, from which I learned I was placed on a performance review plan. The humorous part of all of this was that I was given five accounts the company lost before I was hired. My manager, who was the overall sales manager, informed me that she had called on these accounts for over a year and could not gain one referral. It took me thirty days to gain one referral from all but one of those accounts.

After this ride, my "two-hour ride-along wonder" trainer wanted to place me on an improvement plan. This was her first day on the job. I hope you see how this is a great example of not using proper accountability actions.

A trainer must be able to demonstrate properly and successfully so the employee can learn and repeat or react in the same manner. If the trainer cannot demonstrate correctly, then retraining is needed until the trainer can perform the task, not accountability.

If the trainer cannot demonstrate, a different trainer is needed. Accountability is a tool to change behavior or reward behavior, not to fire employees for giving it their all. A company is not in business to fire employees; it exists to help grow production by growing employees. In chapter 6, we saw how production, service, and safety are taught and unravel when a new employee fills in for a regular employee. Again, if an employee chooses not to do the job when they first demonstrated that they could, then accountability will show them the door in one way or another. Most of your employees want to do a good job and to be paid for it. Use accountability to recognize, reward, and encourage; and you will find you will have little need for negative discipline. In addition, patience will serve you and the company well. Give new employees the proper amount of time to be caught up to speed. How many multimillionaires joke about being fired? What would have happened if the companies from which they were axed were patient instead of quick to fire these future millionaires? You will read later in the book about Jack Welch and how his upper-level manager practiced patience. In brief, Jack provided GE with a huge return based on his manager's patience.

In summary, accountability is good. It forces a good manager or leader to look at data, observe the employees, and make operational corrections if necessary. It also leads to recognition and rewards. A trainer will recognize if an employee needs retraining, but the employee first must show he or she can complete a task or job before being held accountable. Accountability inspires employees to do their job when their manager or leader shows he or she cares. Employees appreciate knowing they do not have to work harder because someone else is not being held accountable.

Accountability promotes the flow of fairness and balance in the workplace and locks out discrimination. In all my years of management, I had one employee attempt to accuse me of being racist. You would have to know me to understand how the accusation is silly. Due to the seriousness of the matter, my division manager asked me to bring my employee records and come to his office to refute this claim. My division manager asked to see my employee records (he was fully aware I write up anyone and everyone who did not follow training). He looked over the write-up on each employee and handed it over to the accuser's friend to view for himself. The accuser's friend turned to his buddy and said, "Well, Tom may be an asshole, but he's an asshole to everyone in his work area. You don't have a case." Did he have to call me that name? I thought I was a fair person. Employee records and documentation are vital to show the paper trail of proper accountability.

Remember that training is a constant; and safety, service, and production will help a company surpass their customers' expectations. It is safe to say accountability is a large factor of success.

12

Rewards vs. Fear

Nothing great was ever achieved without enthusiasm.
—Ralph Waldo Emerson

Gloria approached me one morning in the building before leaving work. Gloria was a loader for the company who had worked with me several years earlier, as one of my loaders. It was 6:00 a.m., and she had been there since 10:00 p.m. She already ate her breakfast after completing her Olympic safety circuit, which was part of my Olympic creativity program aimed to change the poor safety awareness and injury results we encountered in a previous operation. On this day, breakfast was prepared by the division manager and his staff, per the division manager's request. The employees loved when the upper-level managers cooked for them. It was clear that all employees and management had a lot of fun this day.

This event created greater awareness of the importance of safety in our workplace. Our goal was to complete one year without a lost time due to an injury. Gloria was a longtime employee of the company and rarely spoke with management. Therefore, when she approached me and wanted to talk, I knew something was important to her. Gloria said, "Wow, Tom, all of this rewarding is going to break the company. Besides, I am not used to all of this. You even have the big bosses cooking." I knew this was her way of saying thank you. I smiled and said, "You deserve it, Glo. You work hard, and you do an incredibly good job for our company." I told her how the division manager and his staff volunteered to cook. She told me how surprised she was and cool she thought it turned out. Then she asked me nicely how we could afford to feed over one hundred employees, give away T-shirts, and have two mountain bikes in a raffle for the employees. I asked her if she accomplished the seven-circuit safety course. She said yes. I asked her if she felt she had a lesser chance of being injured doing her job since she understands the proper technique. She said yes and that she felt better trained. I told her that knowing she felt this way and went home safely each day was a higher price than paying for all the rewards. Gloria, along with other employees, asked if we were going to do this safety contest again in the future. After that day, many employees became excited about safety training since it was both learning and rewarding. One year later, we all accomplished one year without a lost-time injury.

Success breeds success, and positivity breeds positivity.

That same day, Gloria joked and asked me if I remember her being the "Queen for the Day." I told her she was my first recipient of the award. The "Queen for the Day" was an award system I designed to reward the loader on a belt who loaded the most freight per hour. I rigged a piece of rectangular cardboard to hang from the overhead pole and made it look like a marquee. I wrote in black marker "Queen for the Day" on one side and "King for the Day" on the other. I punched two holes in the top and looped wire through to hang on a pipe in the ceiling. I placed it at the beginning of the belt where all the employees could see the person sitting below the sign. I placed a beanbag chair underneath the sign for the winning employee to sit in. I bought them a soda and either a candy bar or a bag of potato chips for their snack. I gained permission from my manager and the union steward before implementing the idea. My manager loved it, but the union steward had one concern because my supervisor would have had to do the employee's work for ten minutes, while the employee sat and relaxed for additional break at the end of the ten-minute break. I explained how the employee was still on the clock and was not being replaced or asked to punch out. This was just a way to reward them for performing the best in their work area. He said it was a cool idea and asked again if there was another employee who could do the rewarded employee's job for an hour while that employee relaxed. I explained how it was a skilled position, and my supervisor used to load the same area before being promoted. I explained that I would train him if he agreed to leave his job for ten minutes to perform the other employee's task. He looked at me with an expression on his face that he would rather eat rocks for ten minutes. In the end, he approved and asked his supervisor when he was going to implement the idea.

I asked Gloria if her supervisor still offered this reward for her work area, to which she frowned and replied, "No!" I reminded her of the "Queen for the Day" reward as well as the T-shirt and breakfast reward for completing the safety circuit. I also reminded Gloria of being entered in the drawing for a mountain bike. I asked her whom she would rather work with, her current supervisor or me? She chose me but added, "You are not easy to work for." I laughed and asked her what she meant by that. She said that I expected everyone to do his or her job and that I did not favor one employee over another. I asked her if she wanted me to favor anyone. She said no, she liked working with me and really missed the rewards. Then Glo said, laughing, "Okay, you could have favored me a little." Hey, she is human. I was honored to work with Gloria.

I really listened to Glo. I realized she liked how I was fair and expected the same from everyone. The job was tough, but the rewards made it a little more enjoyable. I liked Gloria as an employee. She was hardworking and did her job well every day, and she did not demand a lot from anyone. She tried to get along with everyone, which made her a good person to work with. I am glad she remembered and enjoyed the rewards I put in place. I like to have fun at work. I like to hold people accountable and reward those who earn it. I like to see hardworking people smile at their own accomplishments. I will always remember Glo smiling while she sat in the "Queen for the Day" chair. I do not know who enjoyed the moment more, her or me. In addition, she inspired Dwight, another fellow employee, to achieve the chair reward; and he had just as big a smile on his face. I love how rewards make a person feel appreciated.

Although this is a great example of how rewards motivate success, some may ask, "Doesn't fear work better than rewards?" Besides, fear costs less and saves company money.

Back in chapter 6 on training, I remarked how a bad attitude is the highest cost to a company. I was assigned an operation where the employees did not acknowledge or appreciate their supervisor or management. The employees did not trust or like management people and would not look their way when the manager or supervisor approached. This operation was the worst of its kind in three states. The number of customers' packages left over after the operation was complete resembled bees on a beehive. Management had to help make service for their customers.

A bad attitude in a workforce will create more work injuries. It will cause more service failures, decreasing the reputation of a company due to disgruntled customers. It will cause a slowdown in production that can potentially cost a company tens of thousands of dollars or more.

Fear in an employee will lead to the development of a bad attitude. Fear is a short-term solution to a long-term issue. Inducing fear has shown to motivate employees to work for thirty to forty-five days, but after this period, they will start to see inequalities in the so-called justice. They will start to figure out systems to work around the penalty in place. They will grow tired of the fear, which will most likely turn into resentment. The employees will develop a bad attitude knowing no one cares about them as a person; they will see themselves just as a number or workhorse to management. If they do not feel cared for, they will not care. They will form an interior cohesion against the exterior force. Vince Lombardi knowingly created this kind of fear in the Green Bay players as the head coach. He wanted his men to fear his wrath in order to create inner cohesion within the team. He was willing to be the bad guy to bring his players closer together. He knew this teamwork was imperative for the team and each player to become a champion.

I feel the only place for fear is when watching a scary movie or in a nightmare you cannot wake up from. There is no place for fear in the workplace. Respect is different from fear. I am more of a Tony Dungy kind of leader. If you do not know who Tony Dungy is, you should. He is a great person, a Hall of Fame coach, a record setter, and an overall good-natured person. I suggest that you read about how he led his men to achieve success. Read how he affected the organizations he worked in. I have no doubt you will learn at least one influential lesson from him.

No one should have to work in fear. Work is a means to an end. It helps us acquire what we need whether it be to eat, sleep, and play or have shelter, toys, travel, and retirement. Work is designed to give us a purpose and a part in making life more enjoyable. Work allows us to help others and offers us the chance to develop a service heart. Work is not life itself, but a small part of life. Who are the bosses, dictators, emperors, and dynasties using fear for production? One who strongly comes to mind in recent history is Hitler. Would you want to work for him? How would you like to work for Joseph Stalin? Would you want to work for Genghis Khan, Attila the Hun, Saddam Hussein, or Kim Jong-Il? Anyone in their right mind and given this as an option would decline a job offer from those people without hesitation. Those people used fear as their primary means to gain cooperation.

Fear stifles creativity. It creates a one-track mind, which prevents an employee from doing a quality job. An employee cannot focus on creativity when they are worried about their job or being embarrassed. Their mind is forced to think of job security, but this creates a distraction and hinders an employee from doing their job and doing it well. It reduces their desire to offer suggestions for improving specific processes. Anyone in business long enough will tell you how employees are the ones who come up with ways to improve the process, the job, or the company. If employees fear their manager, trainer, or leader, they will not like them and, thus, will not want to help them.

Now, let us turn our attention to the more positive motivator: reward. Rewards are awesome! First, rewards make a deserving person feel good about what they have accomplished. Therefore, rewards are just.

Second, rewards keep employees on the proper track of job performance. If an employee is rewarded, they receive reinforcement that what they are doing is good. If some form of a reward or recognition is not given, there is a strong chance the employee will feel they are not appreciated, or they are not performing the right way. What happens if employees decide to slow down production? What would happen if the employees were to stop doing well?

Third, rewards create fun in the workplace. Who does not want to have fun? It gives the other employees a chance to tease the winner in a fun way or congratulate them. Hence, it breaks up the monotony of a workday. When I was an operations manager in construction, Peter was a new employee and, therefore, the slowest. Peter worked awfully hard to learn the job and to work faster with better quality and safer. One day, I created two contests for my crew out back of the office. One contest was how fast each employee could install signs on posts, while the second was how fast they could dig holes to place the signposts. Peter won the first sign-installing contest only four months after he was hired. He was so proud to receive a $25 gift card and joyfully spoke about his victory for three days. This clearly boosted his morale so much he told his family as soon as he returned home.

In addition to generating a humble pride, rewards allow the employee's family and friends to congratulate him or her and take pride in them. This creates hope for other employees in the workforce that they can achieve a reward as well. It also reminds the employees of how important their job is to the customers. A company is willing to spend money to reward their employees for good results. Rewards make the standards clear and create an incentive in the workplace for others to behave appropriately and work hard like the rewarded employee. It offers an understanding of the performance to be rewarded. This understanding often compels others to be inspired to achieve their goals. Perhaps, most importantly, it shows employees that their leaders care about them as people.

You may be shocked to learn I was admonished for giving this $25 reward to Peter. My manager (I will call him Larry) in the construction industry told me he thought this was too much of a reward. He told me I should have run this by the owner before I made such a decision. I am not kidding you. My thought was twofold. One, if the owner does not believe a good employee is worth a $25 reward, the company is in serious trouble. Second, if my manager and owner do not trust me to make a $25 decision, why in the world am I running a division of the company worth millions of dollars? In fact, the company was struggling to keep employees and make money. This was related to how they treated, trained, and rewarded their employees. In fact, they did not perform any of these actions well, if any at all.

To further emphasize how important rewarding good employees can be, this company was turned down by eleven of twelve insurance companies for fleet coverage. The owner told me that the workers' comp insurance was so expensive, they may have to self-insure next year. The company turnover was over 67 percent, yet training and rewarding employees was not seen as important. I am confident you do not wish to experience 67 percent turnover in your company and have insurance carriers telling you they will not insure your company. Training your employees properly is a much less costly and more effective manner to reduce these issues.

Years ago, when I worked as a new manager, an older wiser manager told me that if you reward a little too much, you are going to be out of a little money. But if you reward too little, you are out a lot of money. His point was that the employees would work as hard or harder if you reward them. They will slow down or leave if they are not rewarded and do not feel appreciated. Remember, you want people in and outside of your company to *want* to work for you.

The company above is an actual company. The ownership, including the children of the owner, used fear as their number 1 motivator. I cannot tell you how many times they told good managers, employees, and me, "If you can't do your job, I'll find someone who can." I wanted to ask them nicely, "Doesn't this just show that your hiring skills are horrible?"

The people who owned this company hired the employees themselves, so if over 67 percent were terrible, why did they hire them? They were not terrible employees. These employees, including myself, wanted to do well. In fact, in many areas, we did do very well. When one considers that there was little, if any, reward for employees, we all did quite well. I spent a few hundred dollars on rewards in the form of lunch, gift cards, and donuts. I made over $500,000 more and reduced expenses compared to the manager before me in the first six months of the year. Would you accept this trade-off as an owner?

The best endorsement I can give to positive leadership style is the fact that I have always been number 1 in every operation I have worked out of all the companies I have worked in. I have always used reward systems for people whom I have worked with and those who worked under me. The key is make the goal(s) clear to all, achievable, and fair. By doing this, you will have great success, and people will want to work for you. The question title to this chapter is "Reward vs. Fear," so can you see why rewards are so much more effective than fear? Who says work cannot be fun?

13

Accomplishments

You are never too old to set another goal or to dream a new dream.
—C. S. Lewis

I took over a loading operation in early March of 1987 in my first-ever supervisor position. I had always been the employee, and now, I had to think like a leader. I was responsible for seven direct report employees. My job included opening the building at 4:00 a.m., working until 9:00 a.m., and then finishing paperwork so I could leave by 10:00 a.m. I was also finishing my senior year of college, so after work I attended class until 2:00 p.m. To add more on top of that, I coached college football in the afternoon as an undergrad coach. As a former college football player, I liked competition and helping players get better.

Three days into my new career, I discovered a company report I liked. It was a list of operations ranked by production results throughout our state. I was surprised but saddened by the fact that the operation was ranked in the middle of this list. I was curious about how my crew would feel about this and deeply analyzed that night which way would be best to present this information to them. The next day, I asked the team where they felt they *would* rank compared to other employees in the state. Most assured me they would be number 1, while one or two said they thought they would not be ranked any lower than number 2. I showed the employees where we ranked and asked how they felt about it. They were as shocked as I was. Obviously, we all wanted to be number 1, and several employees asked me what this would take. I explained how they needed to do the job in the planned hours allowed for each day, which were based on the volume of freight we processed. I explained how I could calculate the estimated volume each day and let them know when we needed to have the operation completed and everyone off the clock. This would match planned hours with actual hours and rank us in the state operation list. I assured them I would help ensure they had all the tools they needed to be successful.

After setting this as our team-oriented goal, we performed at the number 1–rated level of operations in the state for an entire month. Twenty days later, we obtained this goal. We were the best in the entire state, and I could not wait to show everyone the results and the list with our name highlighted at the top after the rankings were finalized. I also looked forward to having the employees suggest new goals or make suggestions for continuing our success. I was so proud of everyone, but I was not prepared for the comment from a lead employee after obtaining this extremely exciting and worthy accomplishment.

When everyone was done cheering and clapping, and I was still smiling and congratulating the team, one of the longest-tenured employees spoke up. What he said vibrated through my body. It struck my soul like a drink of sour milk strikes the taste buds. He said, "Good. Now, we have accomplished our goal. We can get back to staying on the clock a little longer and making more money." I wanted to yell out, "No!" But I knew the goal would become mine and not the team's if I reacted in a rash manner. I knew I had to remain calm and keep my message simple. I told the team how I was proud of them and that "now, the entire state can see who really the best is." However, like in sports, when you win the Super Bowl, NBA Championship, Wimbledon, or the Masters golf championship, others will try to overtake you. Just ask Tiger Woods. I asked the team if they wanted to be a one-month wonder and go back to a position less than the best or keep working continuously to maintain that number 1 spot.

Most of the employees wanted to remain number 1, obviously. A few said they wanted to stay on the clock longer and increase their pay. I explained how doing the job within the allotted time is what is expected of all of us. I explained how the extra five to ten minutes on the clock per day equated to $3–5 more per week, which equated to the cost of a sandwich. I suggested I bring in donuts, pizza, subs, or something of this nature on Friday if we all did our job the right way. The team liked the idea of donuts at break time on Friday, so we made a deal, and I stuck by it. We remained the number 1 operation in the state for a record twenty-six weeks, a record that still stands today. Granted I had to up the reward to breakfast after a couple of months, it was a fun way to reward the team for our accomplishment. Besides, it brought us closer as a team of people working for the same goal.

You have accomplished your goal. Now, what is next? You can choose many directions for your next step. Before you choose, make sure you fully celebrate the accomplishment, acknowledge those who made it happen, and celebrate the moment without pushing the next challenge in your team's face before they are done celebrating.

You and your team have accomplished one of the most important characteristics of success: knowing and believing that you can be successful.

There will be employees who feel compelled to ask you what the next goal is during the celebration. Tell them you will all sit together and discuss new goals the next day or week as a team, but for now, you want them to enjoy the moment. If you push a new goal while still celebrating the first accomplishment, it changes the success from being about them to being about you. It is not about you—it is about more than you. It is about the company and the team.

Once the well-deserved celebration is over, schedule a time when the entire team can meet. Ask the team members what they feel made the team successful in the last accomplishment. Ask them what goal or accomplishment they would like to achieve next. You may have to give them guidelines, such as customer service goals, production goals, research and development goals, programming goals, etc. I know you will be pleasantly surprised to hear what your team has to say.

I have found that many people like a challenge. A challenge forces employees to feel like they are good at what they do. I have also realized that most employees like to set records and accomplish goals the company may not have thought possible.

It is critical that the team prepares as many aspects and factors of the goal as possible to create ownership and responsibility. The team will feel it is attainable and will want to accomplish the goal rather than just do a task because their manager told them to do it. If it takes a work group months or even a year longer to achieve their goal, what is this compared to years of struggle?

One warning to keep in mind: do not allow your team to set too high of a goal. Once they achieve success, they will try to make a huge statement. Their confidence will be at a high level, and they will feel they can accomplish anything. This is where your leadership is needed. Steer the team toward an achievable goal. Inform them if a goal is too lofty. Explain why it is important to eat it in two bites or more instead of one. This will prevent your team from losing motivation when they fall short of a difficult or even unattainable goal. You can keep the momentum going by setting realistic goals and coaching your team properly to achieve them.

If you want to have fun, tell the team to choose two goals. One goal can be oriented for the area that the team is responsible, and the other goal can be something they think the company should improve on. The second goal can often lead to interdepartmental teamwork and cooperation. If you feel it is a good goal and one that would help the company, you can be the one to approach the other department manager(s) and gain cooperation. When this happens, not only are you going to make the company better, but also the amount of excitement and energy you will create can positively change the company's culture forever.

If I were asked what company-wide goal I would like to see improve within my current company, I would choose training. A company I previously worked with relied completely on each operations manager to complete training of all employees in their store. It sounds good on the surface, but it is not practical. I have seen too often that training is almost nonexistent by the managers. After working in six different locations, I noticed that I was the only one following the original training I received in a two-day orientation class. We were all told how to greet and interact with each customer in our store. We were given five mandatory points to complete with each customer. However, the managers did not even follow these protocols. The only training I witnessed most often was verbal, and it was presented whenever an employee made a noticeable error regarding cash. When I spoke to my manager at the time about the disregarded training practice, they mentioned it only once to the employees and never followed up. I talked to my district manager (my manager's manager) about how we were straying away from obtaining our number 1 goal. The district manager mentioned to my manager how important the five-point greeting was to complete, and the manager agreed. A day later, it went to the wayside, again.

Finally, I called and left a message for the director of operations to call me back on an important matter. He never called me back. I called and asked the COO (chief operating officer) if I could speak with him about it. He passed me back to the director. He again never called me back. Finally, I called the CFO (chief financial officer) who said he had time for me to come in and speak with him about my concern, finally. I knew I was committing career suicide, but I knew I did not want anything to do with staying in this company. I explained how poorly both employees and management were performing and not focusing on several goals. He told me he appreciated my time and took ample notes. He said he would follow up with each person. He asked me what it would take to keep me at the company. I replied if we fixed these issues, this would be a good start. However, after a month plus, I did not hear a thing, nor was there any follow-up. If this were my company, I would look to sell quickly. The other option would be to promote people like myself who care enough, or care at all, and reassign other employees. I felt like the words of a Tom and John Fogerty's (CCR band) song, "There's a place up ahead and I'm going, just as fast as my feet can fly. Come away, come away if you're going, and leave the sinking ship behind."

When a team, department, or organization accomplishes a goal, do not make the mistake of thinking the employees overlook other areas that need improvement. Allow the team to make suggestions. Write them down on a board and ask the team to vote on the one they think should be accomplished first. The second and third goals can be written down and placed in a computer file for the next plan of action. The point: if you believe in your people, they will not disappoint you. Yes, I am aware there are one, two, or maybe even a couple of employees who are not going to care. However, my experience has taught me that when a team is in a room and working on a plan together, excitement builds and makes the noncaring employees see that their peers do care. They realize it is more than just management who cares. This tends to change their attitude and help them understand what is needed to belong in this employee-created culture. Typically, these noncaring employees either get on board or leave.

Now what do you do after accomplishing your goal? Celebrate! Then huddle up and make another goal. Here are a few examples of goals you can set out to accomplish:

1. Set a new company record.
2. Become a showpiece operation.
3. Create a new product or service to improve the company.
4. Accomplish 99 percent accuracy in quality without one error.

5. Discover a book for everyone in the department to read, which will greatly improve the creativity or skill of the work team.
6. Discuss which other department would be best to team up with to most improve the company, and then approach that department's head.

These are just a few simple ideas to demonstrate how other goals are waiting to be accomplished. Never fear that accomplishing a goal will prompt the team to relax too much. Remember, as stated before, success breeds success, and everyone likes to feel part of a successful team.

Last, but certainly not least, was/is there an employee or two who was/were most instrumental in the team's success? If so, can you promote them to a leadership role?

14

Overproduction

> There is virtue in work and there is virtue in
> rest. Use both and overlook neither.
>
> —Alan Cohen

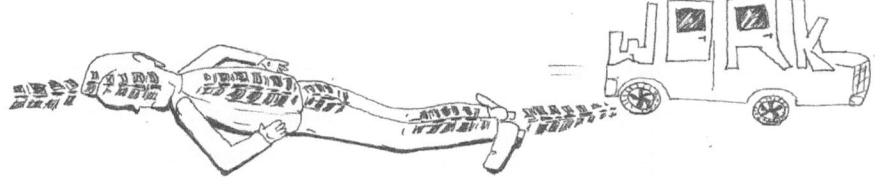

Jerry Kramer is a former All-Pro offensive guard for the Green Bay Packers. Jerry has been inducted into the Packers Hall of Fame as a player, and there is a movement to get him into the NFL Hall of Fame. (Jerry has since been inducted into the NFL Hall of Fame, and rightly so.) Jerry is also an author, speaker, and leader. He may be best known for his block on the Dallas Cowboys defender, Jethro Pugh, allowing quarterback Bart Starr to run a "quarterback sneak" play into the end zone to win the 1967 NFL Championship game, which has come to be known as the Ice Bowl. I have seen numerous pictures of Jerry and other teammates carrying Coach Lombardi off the field on their shoulders.

MORE THAN YOU

It is not Jerry's block I want to point out, but how his manager (in football, this person is called a coach) prepared him for that moment. Coach Vincent Thomas Lombardi is one of the most quoted and recognizable names in coaching today. He led his team (Green Bay Packers) to three consecutive championships and five championships in seven years—a record that still stands today. Coach Lombardi was a leader, and he was voted as the number 1 coach in the history of NFL football by current NFL coaches. He was demanding but knew when to not demand too much. He knew how to prevent burnout.

Jerry once told a story about a day at practice when Coach Lombardi pulled him off the field. He told Jerry to go over to the sideline and think about the block he missed and the way he was practicing. Jerry knelt alongside his teammate, Fuzzy Thurston, and told him, "If the Old Man [Coach Lombardi] yells at me one more time, I'm going to punch him in the mouth." Time went by, and Coach Lombardi yelled to Jerry to come back onto the field and see him. Jerry recalled thinking that he was going to be yelled at again and he was going to hit Coach Lombardi. Thus, he would be fired from the team.

This is the important point of the story: Coach Lombardi put his arm around Jerry's shoulder and his hand on the back of his neck and said, "You know you can play better than you are today. You are better than that. You can be an All-Pro in this league. Now, get back in there and show me what you can do." Jerry said he felt like he could run through a wall at that point and ended the day with a solid practice.

As a manager or business owner, you are a coach. You have people working for you to move the company forward, just like players on a football team attempt to move the ball forward on the field. The players need a coach to bring the best out of them. Likewise, employees need a leader, manager, or owner to encourage them to be their best. A coach, like a manager or owner, has a vision of how he needs his team to play. He or she works at the training process daily to make sure the employees are doing their tasks properly and effectively in order to be successful. Just as Coach Lombardi did with

Jerry Kramer, you must also hold your people accountable, train and encourage them, but do not burn them out.

A great manager, owner, or leader knows how far to challenge his or her employees but does not burn them out. When I was young, I was taught to work hard but give yourself a break after a couple of hours of strenuous work. When I became older, companies I worked for did not have this mindset but instead related breaks with laziness. The one facet I have noticed in the different companies I have been a part of these past thirty years is the high pressure for production. Years ago, people worked hard but were not ridiculous or inhumane about giving some employees some sort of "recovery time." Many businesses were small; and the owners, managers, or supervisors knew not to overwork their employees. This resulted in success and growth for many companies.

I do not spend a lot of time writing on production for the simple fact that many companies know the process that leads to productivity very well. The reason is the productivity is seen as the best or easiest way to save money. I have shown, in chapter 7, how safety is the best and longest-lasting way to save money. When the same employees are present to perform the job by the methods the company has developed for each task, they will become productive. This is due to the employee having time of repeating the tasks. With time comes repetition, and with repetition comes speed or productivity. The factor you must develop as a manager or owner is how to make the task a repeated procedure. Once this is established, the only thing that remains is the correct training of the employee in the task.

One last point on productivity: make sure the standard or goal is communicated clearly, and the employee understands exactly what that goal is for them to accomplish each hour and each day. Then all you must do is follow the training process.

A published study shows employees work longer today than their grandparents did years ago or parents. One can argue how older generations did not have the ergonomics and automation we do today, which made labor harder or more tedious. Maybe this is true, but work is work. The human mind and body can only do a task for so long before it becomes tired and wears down.

As a young boy working in the late '70s through the early '80s, my managers would stop me from working and offer me a cold soda, water, or some sort of refreshment. One day, when I was a high school kid, working at Angeli's Supermarket (grocery store), Ed Angeli, the GM and son of the owner, came into the bakery I was cleaning. He told me to stop working, come over, and have a drink and a donut. I asked him why. I know, what was I thinking? Ed told me I worked hard so I could take a break. He stood alongside and enjoyed a pastry and milk with me. We talked about football and softball and laughed a lot. I would work hard for Ed every time I went into work because he showed that he was an exceptionally good man and leader. I could trust Ed. I knew he liked me and my work ethic, and this made me want to work harder for him.

I joined my first corporation in the mid-1980s, which was all about production and low cost toward providing service. As employees, we were told to take a break. However, once I joined the supervisory team, I do not recall anyone handing me a soda or telling me to take a break. Even as a supervisor or manager, the only time we took a break was when the union employees took a break. Even then, we would have a quick update meeting or walk the work area for progress observations—not an actual "let your mind and body relax" break.

When comparing the difference in work styles, I have come to realize that larger companies are not personable with their employees. They do not know, or take the time to know, employees on a personal level. Corporation CEOs must answer to shareholders (people who buy stock in the company) why the stock did not give them more dividend payout or grow in value. It has become a game of "give me more"; but no one wants to admit how pushing people too far can cause injury, fatigue, absenteeism, and, the costliest aspect, "loss of good attitude" of the employees.

I realize many companies are moving toward automation and robotics for repetitive tasks, but actual humans will always be needed in one facet or another. I hope you will remember the earlier lessons in the chapters of this book, such as the principle of primacy, and about hiring the right people, training properly, communicating properly, using accountability, and working as a team. Do not forget to treat your people well and offer breaks to prevent burnout.

I want to challenge you to own, manage, and lead your people as if they are your family. Treat them as you would want someone to treat your brother, sister, mom, or dad. Having this mindset will allow you to be productive without pushing too hard and losing good employees due to burnout. In every production situation, there is a "law of diminishing return"—a point where trying to gain more production will result in less production. It does not matter if we are using animals, people, or robots; there is a point where the producer is being asked to do more than they are capable. Be a great leader and take the lesson from Coach Lombardi and *know when to pull back and encourage rather than push and dispirit*. Remember, your employees are people. No one wants to fail. This understanding and reasonable approach will prevent burnout. Burnout occurs when a person becomes tired, physically or mentally, from working either too hard or too long at a task. When other managers are losing their heads and telling you to push your employees, remember Rudyard Kipling's quote:

> If you can keep your head when all about you
> Are losing theirs and blaming it on you.
> If you can trust yourself when all men doubt you,
> But make allowance for their doubting too…

This is the first paragraph to Kipling's "If" poem. If you have not read it, you will do yourself a great service by doing so. I know you will find yourself referring to the lesson offered by this poem as you traverse through your career.

You will experience a happier workplace, lower turnover, a more positive culture, a more creative culture, and a more successful company if you ask a reasonable amount from employees without overburdening them with too much production demand. As a wise manager once said to me when I was in sales, "It's a marathon, not a sprint." Being successful in business is a marathon. You want to be successful for many years. Those who push their people too hard will end their business at a faster pace, like a sprint.

In my first full-time supervisory role, as an operations supervisor for a package delivery company, I made the mistake of demanding too much from my employees in my second operation's assignment. I was relocated seven hours away from my hometown and placed in an extremely poor production operation. You know the story from an earlier chapter about the least-best operation. I was fair to my supervisors, but I pushed my good employees too hard during the first few months. It was to the point that three excellent female employees and six male employees told me I was too demanding. I came from an operation where I felt the employees worked faster, and therefore, I thought these new employees could and should be performing better. However, although the good employees in my current operation were loading the same amount of freight as the employees in my previous record-setting operation, they were handling more freight. The reason they were handling more freight was because they were receiving packages in their work area that should have been directed elsewhere. Looking back, I pushed too hard and overlooked this error. I did not recognize that my current employees had decent to good attitudes, *and* they had to deal with employees who had poor attitudes. The good employees were receiving excess freight that was missed by the lesser-performing employees who were ahead of them on the belt. Before they could even continue with their job, they had to move the missed freight out of their work area, which initiated unnecessary delays and extra labor. My previous employee group (from the record-setting company) was veteran, and everyone cared about how well they performed the job. Because the veteran group took a lot of pride in their work, they did not miss as many packages. The group performed like a team, which made work easier for everyone.

Thankfully, by the grace of God, my training took hold with my supervisors, the operation improved, and the amount of freight being missed greatly lessened. This gave much relief to my good employees. I also later apologized to several of the employees for being so demanding. I explained I had to get the operation turned around, and I appreciated them and their efforts. Thankfully, they understood. This is just a reminder that most, perhaps all, people want to do well.

However, before the operation did turn around, one of my female employees (let us call her Linda) quit her position on the belt as a loader at the end of one week and transferred via bid to a clerk position within the same company the following week. She wanted out of my area, and I do not blame her. I should have been more understanding. I was able to develop a work relationship with her later. I think the woman who worked ahead of her on the belt helped me by explaining how the operation improved and how I became more personable. A few times, I spoke with Linda and apologized for pushing her and the others so hard. I explained how I felt that all the employees hated us supervisors and managers. She then reminded me of how the previous team of managers would yell and insult them. I told her I hope I never insulted her or others, but she assured me I did not insult them; I just demanded too much. She tried to make me feel better by explaining how she worked the job for a couple of years before I arrived and wanted to get away from this area of the company anyway. I just helped expedite the move. We laughed, and I apologized again. I told her how the employees were doing better and how her friend ahead of her on the belt even complimented me about the turnaround. She told me she and the other woman talked all the time and was happy for everyone.

Do not make the mistake I did. Do not overburden your people and make them want to leave your work area or the company. Train, follow up, retrain, and analyze all the information accurately to make sure you are not demanding too much production. Prevent burnout of employees. Remember, employees are the lifeblood of any company.

On a positive note, I was reassigned to a driver operation with the same company two years later. Every morning, I arrived through the same door and met with a maintenance employee, Ron. As he was getting ready to end his shift, we would stop and talk to each other for three to five minutes before I would head to my office. Ron had an opportunity to become a driver for the company, which would pay better and offer more hours. Ron was trained by a fellow supervisor for several days, but he was not performing well enough. Ron asked the other supervisor and my manager if I could train him. Ron could sense that I learned from my previous mistake and was a more patient and communicative trainer. After training Ron for a couple of weeks, he performed to standard the first two days but struggled the rest of the time. After three weeks of trying, he approached my manager and told him he would like to go back to his old job. When I found this out, I approached Ron and told him he could do this job and not to give up. However, he told me it was too much, he felt too old, and the labor was not worth it at that point. I told him it was a pleasure to work with him regardless of his position. We continued our friendship at work and spoke every morning. I always asked how he and his family were doing and about his favorite sports teams. During our conversations, he always shared a Bible verse with me, knowing our similar beliefs. I appreciated the person Ron was to both the company and me.

A year later, our state received a new district manager, Tom McBride, who ran the entire state for our company. Tom was the kind of manager whom I loved to work with—he was intelligent, kind, encouraging, and funny. Lastly, he did not appear to care if his manager liked him or not. He was confident in his ability. He approached me one day in my office and told me he had positive news for me. Tom was the most personable of all the district managers under which I have worked. He informed me that he always stopped and talked to the maintenance person in every building he enters because they see, listen to, and hear things others do not. One day, he asked Ron who he thought was the best management person, to which Ron replied me. When Tom asked Ron why he felt this way, he replied that I did not see color, just the person. He thought that I was a great trainer, I wanted people to be successful, I was patient, and I cared. Tom asked me how I felt about this. I told him I was not sure about the great trainer part, I have just learned to be patient, but I agreed with Ron on the rest. He smiled and congratulated me and left the office.

People do not want to get up every day and fail at work. People want to be successful. They want to bring home a paycheck. They want to have a good life. Do not do as I did and push too hard. Demanding too much production will cause burnout. Care about your people. When you take care of them, they will take care of you.

In the 1970s, kids in my age group would get excited when someone squealed their tires. Muscle cars (named this due to their powerful engines) could turn their tires so fast, it would cause a squealing sound. We would clap and cheer when a driver of a muscle car smoked by and squealed their tires. We used to call this action a "burnout." When the tires were so burnt out that all the tread was gone, which did not take long, the owners would throw those tires away. People are not vehicle tires. Do not burn them out and throw them away.

Another significant point I want to make—*be careful whom you promote*. Most companies promote the supervisor or manager who gets the most production out of a group. The promotion is deserved if they performed their job the right way and did not use fear or burnout as their one-two punch. Make sure the person you promote is a leader. Make sure they care about all people and not just their friends. Ask to make sure they prioritize the company and not just themselves. Promoting a supervisor or manager for production numbers can be a double-edged sword. Make sure you are getting the right edge.

15

Ego—The Greatest Killer

The ego is not master in its own house.
—Sigmund Freud

One day, I received a call from Gary, the regional manager of the HR of a distribution company, who said he wanted to apologize to me for something. I told him he did not owe me an apology, and I appreciated that he invited me to the regional offices to instruct two safety workshops. He went on to say those workshops resulted in some of the highest numbers of positive surveys he has ever received toward an instructor. I told him maybe someday I could earn the right to work with him, to which he told me was the reason for his call. He called my state and asked to have me reassigned to him. I told him I loved the idea. However, the person whom he spoke with told him I was not available because I was too valued in the district. I thanked Gary for the call and his effort, but I knew my end was coming soon because I did not want to work for a company that was going to hold me back from earned opportunities to grow and earn promotions. I was mentally preparing to leave soon, which I did three years later.

After this conversation, I thought back to the time I spoke with a corporate manager I worked with in R&D for the company. He and I worked together for seven months—we worked together like peanut butter and jelly. We saw eye to eye and agreed that what was best for the company must come first over personal wants. He was a great mentor to me, and I appreciated his guidance in our time working together. One day in 1992, I received a phone call and was elated to recognize one of my old mentors, Dr. Steven Thompson, right away. He asked me how I would feel about being assigned to him and traveling the country to implement automated hubs for the company. I told him I would love it, but I reminded him I would have to call my spouse and make sure she was fine with the idea. Steven told me he was flying to my hub to check on how things were progressing and would talk with my district manager and attempt to get his permission. I was walking on a cloud. Yes, the money would be great, I would have had more shares of stock in the company, and I would have had more of an effect on the company. However, the aspect of this promotion that pleased me the most was working with a great person, mind, and mentor, Steven.

Little did I know the ego would come out of the cloud like a lightning bolt and shoot the promotion down. I never found out who exactly declined the idea, but Steven told me the district manager said a couple of his staff said no to it. Steven and I were both upset about the decision. This came back to me when I got off from the phone with our regional manager, Gary. I knew I would not be happy staying in the company with people who could not control their egos. Didn't they know who I was?

My own ego got in the way.

I left the company in frustration three years later. I left a company where I had four weeks of vacation, made a solid income, and received stock in the company, which was more valuable than my paycheck. In addition, I had good benefits. What was I thinking? My ego stepped in, and I stepped out. Life happens for a reason, but my ego forced something to happen, which affected more than me. My family was affected as well. I had to relocate my family out of the area for my new job to a new town that was seven hours north of my current town. My kids were going into third and fifth grades, and the move took them away from their friends. My wife had to leave her job as a teacher, which she greatly enjoyed. My ego negatively affected those I love. I affected the friends we had for ten years since we had to move out of the area for my new career. I affected the schools in the area, as well as the church we belonged in. We moved from an area of the state where there was less snowfall to an area with greater snowfall. We had a shorter spring and summer. I caused life to be harder in every phase. The one blessing was that our immediate families lived in our new town.

I was immediately hired by a pharmaceutical company, Parke-Davis. I really loved this company and its people. They took particularly good care of their people. They flew me to Chicago for an interview and picked me up in a limousine. They flew me back home, and I was hired the same day. My kids now lived in the same town as their grandparents. Unfortunately, my mother-in-law, Gina, passed from bone cancer within a few years of us moving back. She was a saint and did not have a known enemy, and my kids and I loved spending time with her. A couple of years after her passing, I then lost my father to cancer. He was also a saint loved by everyone. Despite the negativities of my job loss years earlier and the move, it allowed my kids and me to spend quality time with my dad before his passing. We now have very fond memories of those times.

With my new job, I was assigned to a great partner, Dennis, to share the territory where I happened to be born and raised. He had been doing the job almost fifteen years when I joined him. He won many awards and was a legend in the company before I came along. I had played high school and college sports, and several friends I grew up with were now physicians in the area. My partner and I set records and achieved a lot of success. We were the life of the party at district and national meetings. He played the banjo, and I told jokes. Looking back on it, we should have taken the show to Vaudeville. One night, he played his banjo for two hours at a large resort where we were staying for a regional meeting. He played in the atrium as a few of us sales reps enjoyed his skill on the strings. Soon, there were about thirty reps and other hotel guests who were not part of the conference gathered around, listening and enjoying the music. On a different night, my partner introduced me to a friend of his, a fellow rep from the Detroit area. I found his friend to be a funny sarcastic type of person. I find there are two kinds of sarcastic: the negative sarcastic and the funny sarcastic. His friend and I took turns telling jokes for over two hours at the bar that evening. We had twenty to thirty reps standing around us in a circle and laughing hysterically. I do not know if I have ever had such a great time at a meeting.

The next day, I performed a sales pitch (we called it detailing) to my manager and peers. The company was having a contest to see who the best detail rep was in the region. They videotaped all our sales pitches, or details. I beat out the five hundred reps in the region for first place and received a plaque and $500. The company did it again six months later, and again, I won. This was the first-ever contest of its kind in the company, and I won back-to-back attempts. I did not see the ego coming again, but it hit me like a semitruck grill smashing a bug.

Parke-Davis was a company most anyone would want to work in. They had great managers, leaders, and employees. This company respected its people. Everyone was on a first-name basis, even our president, John Hall. The first time I met John, he called me by my first name. I was honored. I called him Mr. Hall. He smiled and reminded me that our company policy is everyone is on a first-name basis. Later, Parke-Davis was bought out by a conglomerate pharmaceutical company. I have nothing against this company or its people, as it is a successful and admired company. They have particularly good leadership and an excellent training program for the sales force.

MORE THAN YOU

Sometime later, as part of a different pharmaceutical company I worked for, the manager I received as my direct report just did not like me. I want you to understand, we had never met before. We did not know each other, nor had we ever worked together. This is how I found out he did not like me. He called for all the reps under him to report to a district meeting a week after he was assigned to our group. In the very first meeting he conducted, he asked all of us who the best sales rep was in our opinion. My peers asked a few questions: Do you mean in the company? Do mean in our region? Do you mean among us? I could tell the manager was becoming irritated. He was a short round man who rather reminded me of Winnie the Pooh. His face became red, and his voice rose. "I mean in this group, the group in this room, my sales reps." He finally decided to go around the room and ask each one of us individually. My peers called out different people, but most said my name. I was starting to feel embarrassed and had a bad feeling about his motives. I had met people like him before in life, and I anticipated that his ego would be bruised, and I would garner his wrath. I wanted to go to the concierge and check the calendar to make sure I was still living in 2003. When the question came around to me, I explained I felt Peggy was our best rep. She was a nurse and had amazing experience and knowledge of the disease states. I think he liked my answer, so I thought I avoided his bullet of anger. When everyone answered his question and gave their opinion, he stated, "I'm the best rep in this room." My mind went back to a scene in the movie *Stripes*, one of my all-time favorite movies, with Bill Murray and John Candy (rest his soul). In the scene, Sergeant Hulka (played by Warren Oates) tells the new arrival of GIs that he is in charge: "Your mamas are not here to take care of you now. It's just you, me, and Uncle Sam. And before I leave you, you're gonna find out me and Uncle Sam are one and the same." Bill Murray responds, "Uncle Hulka?" If one looks at the cast from this movie, it is one of the best to be assembled. So immediately, relating this moment in time to that movie made me want to say to my new manager, "Uncle Reppy?" Although my ego was big, I was not stupid.

After the manager finished his harsh introduction and listed his expectations, he gave us a ten-minute break. He asked me to meet with him immediately. I swore I saw his ego leave the room ahead of his body. He took me down the hallway and around a corner, and we sat on a bench. He quickly informed me, "I don't like you." Is this a poor way to start a conversation with someone you just met, or is it just me? He went on to say that I must think I am pretty "hot stuff" (*stuff* wasn't the actual word he used), and he was going to "straighten me out." Again, I found this amazing and fascinating how someone who never met me had this feeling toward me. I also was a bit shocked he would talk to his highest-rated rep (number 1 in the region), who was also in the top 7 in the country for my drug portfolio. I wanted to stop him and say, "Stay still. I have a pin, and I think I can pop your ego and save your life." I do not think he would have seen the humor. I asked him what I did to offend him or give him such an impression. I was always told I was polite, cordial, and well mannered. Ego was not a term used in association with my actions. He said he didn't have to meet me, but he knew I needed a lesson, and he was going to get rid of me from this company. I can honestly say I do not know what I did or said to anyone to make him want to get rid of me so badly. I do not think I'm a special person. Well, we are all special in God's eyes, but I do not think I'm better than anyone else is. I usually try to give credit and share success. Even when I won the $500 for the regional detail contest, I gave $100 to my partner. My partner asked me why I was doing this. I explained it was a thank you to him for helping me in my career. He told me I did not need to do it, but I insisted.

 My new manager's ego convinced me to leave the company. I cannot imagine working for someone who hated people so much. I thought it was just me, but I found out he behaved the same way when talking to a few reps later. Here is the funny part about how life works. He called a meeting a month later and asked all of us to bring our families. He brought his son and daughter. My son, daughter, and I were playing catch in the hotel pool after the meeting let out. His son wanted to play with my kids and me when he saw the fun we were having. The manager let his son play with us for a little while, but then his wife showed up and demanded his son to come over to them. Later that evening, we all went to a tree farm to cut our own

Christmas tree—this was an idea our manager came up. I thought it was very cool and told him so. I hoped my compliment would show that I respected him and wanted to acknowledge his idea. His son saw my family get out of the vehicle, and he ran over to us. He begged me to let him join us. I told him we would be happy to have him come along if it was all right with his mom and dad. His dad told him no and to stop crying. I was hoping at the very least, both families could tree shop with each other and make the evening more fun by laughing and joking. As I walked away with my family, all I could think of was how much ego kills joy.

A few weeks later, my sales manager decided he would ride with me one afternoon. His goal was to show me how to do this job better than I was doing it. He was kicked out of two of my offices for being rude. In one office, he mocked the physician who had a Scandinavian accent. I wanted to crawl under a desk when he acted like a two-year-old. The physician told me I was always welcome in his office but to never bring this person back again; he was not welcome. After my manager was asked directly to never come back into the second office, he wanted to talk to me out in the vehicle. He said I was too soft on my doctors and that I had to demand more. Remember, I am top 7 in the country, and usually in the top 5 of that 7. I did not argue with him. I pulled the keys from the ignition; it had been on since it was winter, and the vehicle was cold. He asked me what I was doing. I told him I lived nearby and could walk home. I told him I was done working with him. He wanted me out of the company, and I told him I was going to help him. He continued to tell me how I needed to sell in my territory. I reminded him I was the *only* rep with 100 percent access to all the offices in my territory. I reminded him of my ranking. I lastly reminded him it is exceedingly difficult to sell when you are kicked out of offices, of which he accomplished in three hours. I told him straight out I would not be able to work with someone who was so unintelligent that they would speak down to doctors with the intent of offending them. I told him his ego would cause him a lot of pain in life, and I did not want or need any of it. Two weeks later, I took the offered buyout.

Years prior, it was some egotistical manager in my first company who declined my promotion suggested by the corporate and regional manager to better the company. Now, it was another egotistical manager who wanted to fire me before ever meeting me, which would hurt his company's sales. The same ego manager was hurting his own child by not allowing him to hang out with my kids. He probably prevented my kids from enjoying the holiday evening with a sweet kid.

My next career brought me to one of the fastest-growing insurance companies in the country. I met a man about my age at the state testing office for insurance certificates. We were staying at the same hotel, and we seemingly got along fine. I found out he was joining the same company as I. Later, we went to a twenty-one-day training class at the company's corporate office. Again, we got along fine and conversed when we were not in class. On day 2 of the class, the instructors announced they were creating a competition. We were all competing against each other for "best new employee" in the company. It was a training class award, and the winner would get his or her picture placed on the wall in the board of directors' room. They took us all in the room to see the past winners.

I won the award, thanks to those classmates and instructors who voted for me. Even though we were from the same state and had the same manager, my new friend did not talk with me much after I won. I always felt I could have learned from him while also helping and sharing things I learned and experienced with him. His ego would not allow it.

I was blessed to have played college football when I was younger. I saw men on the team whose egos were so large, they did not want their friends to hang around a specific teammate off the field. I can only guess they feared their friend would like the other teammate and would hang with them, the ego, less. I remember thinking how much better and closer our team could have been if players all went out together or sat around and talked with each other.

Naturally, not everyone will get along with everyone else. Human nature seems to prevent us from always having great chemistry with everyone for an unknown reason. It is because of this fact I feel so badly when someone attempts to foster more actions of divisiveness with teammates, coworkers, or friends. It just does not make sense.

The ego kills relationships.

When I became a senior on my college football team, many of us leaders had a very inclusive personality and behavior pattern. Our coaches were a large part of this mentality as well. I noticed our team was closer and had a better chemistry to it. I felt that when we faced an opponent or gathered on or off the field, we were always a team. We had three players from that team make the NFL, and another player was a standout in the CFL for many years. Two years after I was done playing, a year after I was an undergrad coach, some of my old teammates with new players went to the semifinals in the playoffs. It was the furthest our university had gone in over twelve years. It was due to many reasons, one of which was because the ego was put aside, and the teammates were able to bond and form a close relationship.

In 2010, a startup company hired me as the business development manager. This allowed me to move to Florida and live where I used to vacation. Life was good. I wish I had popped my ego at this point. I grew the company to over $170K in three months. I guess the success changed both the owner and me. He decided to change the plan to not have "weekend calls" for interested prospects. This policy is what had me in the office on a prior Saturday when an important call came in. I received a call from an out-of-state prospect looking for service and care for her mother. I was able to answer her concerns, put her fears to rest, and secure the contract. The day the owner had made the decision to stop returning calls to prospects on the weekend, I was out in the community working. He informed me of this new policy when I came into the office. This offended me because he assured me he would discuss marketing and business development ideas with me before making drastic decisions. This agreement was established my first day on the job. I always assured him he was the owner and had my utmost respect. I acknowledged all decisions were his to make but asked him to allow me to share ideas in the area of my expertise before making a final decision. This would offer him the most information to make the best decision. He promised me he would and agreed that he knew little about marketing and sales. This promise and another major one was broken. I let my ego get in the way of our relationship and business. My ego was bruised, and I made two mistakes that cost me my job. First, I sent him an e-mail telling him I was going to cut back on my effort due to the company looking to reduce opportunities to grow. I would not come in an hour early nor go home two to three hours late. These decisions had a direct effect on my income and bonus. I know, again, what was I thinking?

The next day, the owner asked me to join him in his office. He lied and told me that he found I cheated on my expense account and was going to fire me. I asked him to show me where I cheated on my expense account. The only thing I had on the form was mileage and one luncheon the office could verify. He became flustered and told me I was fired. The second mistake was mixing my ego with his ego, which only induced negative energy.

Egotistical decisions, including mine, are a killer.

This stifled the company's income, growth, and financial happiness. His ego changed the company hours of operation and prevented callers from getting the help they needed. Many prospects were women and men between the ages of forty and sixty years old. They were the ones who were taking care of an elderly parent. They had become burned out and reached out to our company. Thus, this also had a negative effect on patients who needed to find a company like ours to help them. Not being able to call on weekends directed potential clients to other companies, thus resulting in customer loss for the company. What would have happened if I had not let my ego get in the way? Shame on me for allowing that to happen. I also let my ego stifle my income, growth, and financial happiness. I would like to think I am just very principled, but this would be avoiding the truth, which was that my ego got in the way.

I am currently employed by a company that prides itself on customer service. I tried to speak with the director of operations at the first meeting I attended three months after I joined the company. I noticed how our communication format for follow-up training was not effective and resulted in poor customer service, angry customers, and uninformed employees. I tried to speak with him in a question format to state what I observed and ask what he thought about implementing a UPS-used format to communicate before shifts started. He said the company already had their own way of doing it. He explained it was simple—write down a note in a booklet, then the employees are supposed to read the note before starting their shift. Let us review this idea.

The idea I suggested comes from a company that has been rated as high as the fourth most admired in the world by *Forbes Magazine*. My current company is not even rated as best in their region of the country. The idea I had learned worked very well. Other company owners I have spoken to about this love the idea. My current company prefers a method where there is no way to ask a question *if* the information written in the book is only halfway decently written. Usually, no one even wrote anything in the book, and it was placed under the counter to collect dust. The other issue with this method was that employees who were running late or were barely on time did not read the notebook. Don't you love when managers use their egos to squash ideas that would be more effective? I suggested using a person to communicate and take questions, whereas the director would rather use a notebook, where no questions can be asked, and no answers can be offered. The ego strikes again.

I suggested to our lead and the company's only trainer (let us call him Rob), "Telling is not selling, and telling is not training." I stated it more eloquently and less bluntly than I do here in the book. I asked Rob why we do not role-play more and design a more interactive training process for new-hire learning. He responded, "We don't have time for additional training." What, we do not have time to learn the right and more effective way? We have time to teach a new hire truly little and send them out to the job unequipped, but we don't have time to train the person who directly interacts with our customers? I wish there were more ego-killing ideas in this world. We just do not seem to have enough egos to kill every living thing. It reminds me of the funny skit on *Saturday Night Live*, when Will Ferrell is playing in a band and a producer (Christopher Walken) keeps telling the band, "We need more cowbell." I feel like there is some business guru out there in the stratosphere telling decision makers, "We need more egos, ideas are still living, and we must kill them." I have placed my ego on a weight-loss program. I hope other decision makers will do the same.

I was recently at a meeting for a convenience store company. The lead trainer stated the company had zero lost-time injuries for the first quarter. He asked if anyone had ideas to keep this trend going and prevent injury. I waited to hear a few other employees' suggestions before stating mine: "Observation, explanation, commentary, and drill." The trainer asked me to explain what I meant by this. Notice that he did not say, "So the class understands what you mean by this." He simply did not understand or know how to properly train. I explained in brief detail how it is the most effective way to train in a hurry and maximize effectiveness. He thanked me, told me it was a great point, and moved on. I realized he was in front of two hundred people and could not dive further in to get more details about my suggestion. I have been there myself. However, the manager never called or followed up with me to get more information. His ego prevented him to inquire about my idea and receive critical information for growth. Ego prevents learning, which prevents growth and further inhibits companies from growing and becoming more successful. This lack of growth and success leads to local, state, and national economic stagnation. When a country the size of the United States has a stagnated or declining economy, it affects the entire world. It is wild to think an economy can be so greatly inhibited by something we cannot even see it—the ego, the biggest predator of them all.

I recently interviewed with a company, which has retail, fuel delivery, and building material holdings. I first met the division manager (I will call him Jim) at one of his retail locations. He oversees several operation locations. I introduced myself and asked if his company was hiring operations managers, to which he replied they have a manager-in-training (MIT) program. I spoke with him for about fifteen minutes in the back of his store before he told me he liked what I had to say and would call me to set up a face-to-face interview.

Jim did call me. Before the interview commenced and Jim arrived, I spoke with his company's human resources (HR) manager. She was a nice person, as most HR managers tend to be. I think there is an unwritten rule out there: if you cannot hold a friendly half-hour conversation without saying anything pertinent about the company, you cannot be an HR manager. Jim joined us several minutes later. The interview was going swimmingly until I bruised his ego. He asked me, "How long before you become bored as a store manager and would want to do something else?" I explained how I did not see this as a concern for a few reasons. First, I would want him to mentor me so that I could strive to make my store a showpiece for the company, a store that he could take pride in, bring in, and show all levels of managers and executives of the company. Second, I believe it will take time to make the store a showpiece or perfect operation. He seemed fine with these responses. Third, I have been trained well and cross-trained in different companies. I have diverse experience in human resources, operations management, driving across country as a CDL A driver, and worked concrete construction for two summers during college. If he felt the store was a showpiece store and I was ready, perhaps I could move into training, delivery training, or building materials management. This is what appeared to make his face turn a funny shade of red. Ironically, as the HR manager was about to pronounce that this was a good answer, I thought the division manager stepped out and the Kool-Aid man stepped in. You know the Kool-Aid man I am referring to—a big red pitcher of Kool-Aid who busts through the wall in the commercial whenever someone says, "Hey, Kool-Aid." He said something about those areas not needing someone right now, and those were not under his area of responsibility. He told me he had three to four other good candidates for the MIT position and did not think he would have room for me at that time. I wonder why a division manager would waste his and the human resources manager's time with someone whom he does not have room for at this time. Does he think I was born yesterday? I am guessing the murderer of the industry came, choked out his common sense, and left before he could ID him. The ego strikes again. His ego was bruised, and he was angry. I wanted to make him look good until he was promoted regardless of how long this may have taken. The funny thing is I did not say I wouldn't. I told him I would enjoy working with a mentor like him and desired to develop a showpiece store, one that he could proudly show his bosses.

I recall friends of mine reminding me how the ego allows us to take good care of ourselves. Although it can motivate us to succeed, a little goes a long way.

Do I greatly dislike these people? Am I mad at these people? What is wrong with them? The answers to these questions are no, no, and they are human. If no, then why or how am I not mad? I understand that decisions derived from the ego are a result of scared, hurt, or selfish feelings. How many of us feel those feelings at one time or another? I know I have. The difference between others and me is that I have learned it is about more than I am, while they have yet to absorb this.

When my ego tries to kill an idea, a relationship, or business growth, I attempt to reflect on my irrational fear and move beyond it. I try to make decisions that are best for the other person, the company, or our relationship. I am not perfect at this, and I never will be because I am human. However, I have become quite effective at making decisions that have proven to be best for whatever company I am a part of at that time. This primal lesson goes back to my first division manager, Bob Crouch, who told me his number 1 responsibility was the company's well-being. This required finding talented people for the company. I have nearly perfected encouraging a person rather than killing their creativity or good ideas. I continue to improve on preventing others' egos from ending my relationship with them. I cannot always say they *want* to talk with me, but I am open to talk with them and be their friend.

I greatly admire companies that encourage their employees of all levels to be creative and suggest bold ideas. I love hearing companies ask creative questions during interviews and try to get into the mind of the new candidate by keeping an open mind. I have heard that companies like Uber, Apple, Yahoo, Google, Microsoft, and Facebook encourage their employees to share new thoughts and ways of doing business. Dan Price, the CEO of Gravity Payment, took a pay cut because he heard employees who make $70,000 or more per year are financially happy. Dan Price is someone I can admire. He gets it. He knows to put the ego aside and look at those around you. He knows working together, not over or under, and side by side will grow a company. Now, the key is for Dan's employees to give to the company the way Dan has given to them and not become complacent. Dan will have to make sure he measures results and holds each person accountable for their results. Life cannot be a one-way street. If the company gives to employees, the employees must give back to the company. I cannot predict the future, but I would bet Dan has success in both business and life.

I have worked for managers and mentors who were remarkably successful in their company. I found the more successful the manager, the more they were willing to mentor and coach me to grow the company. These managers were leaders, believed in the company first, cared for good people, intelligent, kind, visionaries, and admired by their understudies. I think of good men like Bob Crouch, Steven Thompson, Randy Rand, Chris Carley, Glover Johnson, Garth Goodlett, Dave Sabourn, my brothers (Dan, Mike, Jim, Pete, and Bill), and my son, Thomas Anthony. I think of good women like Holly Cabutto, Donna Tisdale, Meredith Walker, Jennifer Hill, Jane Kuhlman, Nancy Tyree, Fae DePetro, and my daughter, Alicia Fae. All these people are excellent leaders because they do not let their ego get in the way of what is right for a company, employee, fellow student, or friend.

If we care about others, we will make very few, if any, decisions with our ego and make more with our intelligence and our heart. Our head and our heart know what is best for customers, employees, the company, and the individual. We just need to keep the ego out of it.

16

How to Spot a Great Leader

The task of the leader is to get their people from
where they are to where they have not been.
—Henry Kissinger

When I was in college and working at my first "real job," my first division manager (my manager's manager) told me, his main goal for the company, as part owner, was to spot and attract talented people. I initially thought he was wrong. Surely, his first job was to run a profitable business and take care of the customer. However, the more I thought about it and rationalized it out, the more I realized how right he was. If you spot talented people and you attract them to your company, you will make a profit. People (employees and customers) are what determine the profitability of a company. Talented people are valuable because of their skill set, which helps bring success to a company.

What is the difference between a leader and someone who is promoted into a leadership position? Alternatively, is there even a difference?

A distinct difference separates a true leader from others. A true leader is not just a person who occupies a leadership position; they understand that all their abilities come from God, and thus, they care. They understand someone took the time to show them a skill or trade, and they want to pass on this caring attitude to others. True leaders understand that giving, helping, and inspiring others are what they want to do. They do not see this behavior as something they should do, but something they do naturally. Caring enough to want to help others is something they do not even think about; it just happens. It is who they are, not what they do.

While speaking to one of the owners of the best breakfast and lunch restaurant (the Metro Diner) one day, I asked him why he jumps in and helps train his employees. This family-owned diner (mother, father, and their two sons, Mark and Paul) is located throughout the greater Jacksonville area and St. Augustine in Florida. Mark informed me that he jumps in and shows employees how to do something right because he wants them to learn the right way the first time. Mark went on to tell me how long he has also cooked for his own restaurant. He learned from others how to do it better and faster by doing things a certain way. He wants to pass this behavior onto his employees so they can do it better and faster, which is not simply good for business, but also good for the employees. It makes the job easier and more consistent than doing it all kinds of different ways. You get a happier, less stressed employee, a better product or meal, and a more satisfied customer.

Mark does not jump in because he is trying to exhort authority. He knows, as an owner, he has authority. When talking to him, I see he does it because he genuinely cares about the employees and customers (whom he calls family) and about the company being successful, obviously. He genuinely cares about the feelings of his employees. He does not have to think, *Gee, should I take a minute and show this employee something?* He stops and trains as a part of who he is, and by doing so, he is creating a culture of caring within his restaurants. He leads by example, and I have observed his efforts, which are duplicated by his GM. His GM has treated me like family since my very first visit to the diner. He asks questions to ensure I am happy with the food and service, and he clearly just cares.

The owner/manager leads the charge, while his GM demonstrates and trains the employees daily to create this caring and successful culture. The result is an excellent company, which will get my business until I am dead or until they stop caring (which I never see happening). To me, the owners and GM are perfect examples of great leaders.

Leaders have an open mind and open ears. A true leader wants to know why things are going a certain way and what issue is causing things to happen. A leader wants to know what is causing a problem and wants to work with people in solving the problem. He or she also wants to know what portion of the business is going well and how to maintain or enhance it.

I used to tell employees to pick it up or get it going. Now, I know to ask the employee questions to find out why they are not performing the job like they usually do or how they know to do it. I have learned much more from discussions like this instead of by commanding or reprimanding. This helps me to learn whether an employee was trained properly or not. This offers me feedback about the trainers and company culture. Other times, I have learned that something going on in an employee's life may be affecting their performance, and by listening to them just for a moment is enough to show the employee I care.

Many times, just having our leader listen to us is enough for us to improve our performance. I have shared with business owners how I could tell they cared because of how they spoke about their employees as if they were a family member.

Mark has asked me questions about comments I have made about his business, which I had learned from others. On several occasions, he asked me to repeat some of these comments, and then he wrote them down. Many times, he asked me for more details about a concept I brought up and then commented how much he liked my presented idea. This gave me further morale to write this book—to share the ideas handed down to me by people much wiser and experienced than me. I was simply passing what I had learned thus far to him and gladly did so because I could tell he genuinely cared. I promised him I would be happy to do this.

Leaders have open ears and an open mind. When a leader hears a new idea or methodologies that can help them or those who work for them, they take great care to capture and exhibit it. Leaders ask many questions to help them continuously learn to get better. As a leader, I work daily to become better at asking questions. If you practice asking good questions, you are going to be a great leader in your industry. Some leaders have the same characteristics as Jim Casey (founder of UPS). I recall reading stories of others who had met Mr. Casey in their travels and remarked that he asked many questions about what they did for a living. Some stated that by the time they were done talking about their job, Jim was an expert in their industry too.

Leaders never stop listening and learning. When you ask questions, it shows you care about a topic or the person speaking, and by showing you care reveals that you want to learn more because you want to help in some way. When a person cares, they open their ears, mind, and heart and listen to what the other person is saying. When they open their ears and mind, they are learning. Moreover, when a person wants to continuously learn, it becomes a lifelong habit. This is a sign of a true leader—a leader never stops learning, listening, or helping to improve themselves and others. The result from this can only make the world a better place because caring people tend to bring others around them up to a higher level of understanding. Leaders will often continue their studies in a higher education program, such as a master's degree or doctorate.

One day, I was sitting in an operations meeting with several managers. It was customary for this company to meet daily before commencement of the operation and discuss issues, needs, and wants; thus, it was called the preoperation meeting. At the conclusion of each meeting, the manager in charge went around the table and asked other managers if they had something to add. Every manager in the meeting was given a chance to speak. When it came to my turn, I said, "Listen." All the managers, including the division manager, listened. The division manager asked me what he was listening for. No one in the room heard what I heard. I heard money leaving the company from the sound of belts and motors running throughout the building. These belts and motors gave off a humming noise that vibrated throughout the building. I asked the other managers, "You don't hear it?" To which they still responded, "No." The reason they did not hear was because they had been in this environment for six months, so this humming sound became routine to them. I pointed out how all the belts and motors were running at that time. One manager said this was because of a pretrip procedure completed by the supervisors to prevent delays in the operation due to nonworking equipment. I kindly asked them what time it was, to which they replied 2:00 p.m. Then I asked what time the operation began, to which they replied 4:00 p.m. Finally, I questioned why we were pretripping our belts an hour earlier than we should be. At this point, many of their eyes opened wide. They realized our procedure was not being followed correctly. The more interesting part of this story was that I was the youngest manager in that meeting and had the least amount of operations experience. I was after more than just following procedures; I was trying to save us money. I then asked our maintenance manager, Jeff, how much it costs to run the belts, rollers, and motors for one hour. He replied that this is based on volts and watts. He then quickly assured me that we were rated extremely high in efficiency (96 percent) and number 1 in the area by the power company. This made me smile inside my heart because I knew 96 percent could be improved on. I knew I could show our company how to save even more money. Some of the managers reacted to Jeff's comment of us being number 1 as if this were all-important. I asked Jeff if I could get with him immediately after the meeting so he could show me what our watts and volts were running at. Jeff was happy to show me the watts and volts we were using while the belts were running idle without freight. Later that evening when I arrived home, I waited until after my kids went to bed and my spouse was busy, then I called the power company. I asked for our company's cost per volt and amp. I calculated the cost for one hour and verified it by bouncing my calculation with the power company's supervisor. He assured me I was correct. He too assured me we were running with high efficiency. I thanked him for his time and help. The following day, I met with the same managers in our preoperation. Jeff recommended that the group ask me what I found out about our belts running too early each day. I smiled and said we could only save $18.82 per day, which translated to $583.33 per month and $7,000 per year by starting the pretrip an hour later. The other managers were slightly impressed until I reminded them this savings of $7,000 was for each operation, which could save over $21,000 per year in our three operations. I asked Jeff to tell the managers what he told me the day before, and he reminded them that there was zero cost to obtain this money savings. In fact, I told them how Jeff informed me that the more we run those belts and motors, the more maintenance cost we have and the sooner the equipment wears down. In actuality, the $21,000 savings was just the tip of the iceberg. Just like in safety, there are hidden costs associated with this waste. After this meeting, I reminded my fellow managers that they could be the bearers of good news and tell all their supervisors that they could complete the same job by arriving one hour later each day.

When my division manager congratulated me for paying attention and saving the company money, I gave credit to those who mentored me. I thanked Steven Thompson (automation's corporate manager) for showing me the value of stopping, watching, and listening. I thanked the company for training me in industrial engineering, which taught me critical thinking and analysis. I even thanked my family who taught me to turn down the propane heat and save gas when we were away from the trailer during hunting trips. I used all these experiences, both small and big, to reduce our costs. You see, it is about more than you. Leaders listen and learn as they always try to find a way to improve themselves and their company. Mostly, they do this because they care.

The following comment I have stated to several businesspeople who have agreed with me:

"I will hire a mediocre person who shows they care about my company before a talented person who shows minimal amount of care."

When a person cares, it is part of who they are, and it is something that will not change. They will continue to help others. They will want to learn and understand how to get better because they care. A smart person may be smart in a discipline of a business, but if they do not care, they often will not pass their knowledge on to others. I have found often that smart people learn how to make the job easier for themselves but do not care to show others how to do it for fear of losing the edge of being smarter or better. This does not help any company multiply its efforts to grow toward the one common goal, achieving success, which provides job security for everyone.

A couple of coaches in the NFL (National Football League) have proven to be excellent leaders both on and off the field. I have followed Mike McCarthy, head coach of the Green Bay Packers. The Packers are my favorite NFL team since I was old enough to talk. My family followed the Packers before I was born. What impresses me the most about Coach McCarthy is how he rotates his assistant coaches every year to coach a different position than they did the previous year. Sometimes this means an assistant coach is coaching a new position for the first time ever. Coach McCarthy demonstrates his desire to help his assistants become better coaches by learning how each position on the team affects and completes the team goal. The results are a better assistant coach, enhanced player performance, and greater team success. Coach McCarthy is an innovative leader in his approach to coaching. I believe he would say that the reason he does this is he cares as much about the future success of his people (coaches) as he does the success of his team. McCarthy also puts his ego aside for the good of the team. Even before Aaron Rodgers stated this during an interview on May 28, 2015 (Packers.com), I knew this to be true. Aaron's response to a question by a reporter about Coach Mike McCarthy, "First, he has to have a small ego," shows that McCarthy's success comes from relinquishing the play-calling duties of the team or handing over control to his subordinate coach, unless they prove they cannot handle the job. Small ego and success go hand in hand. If you want to win, be successful, earn respect, make a lot of money, and lead people, lose the ego. Look at all the division titles since Mike McCarthy has taken over as head coach of the Packers. Look at the team's Super Bowl title and playoff consistency. The Packers and the New England Patriots are the only teams in this time span to reach the playoffs seven consecutive years. Coach McCarthy is and will continue to be a great leader.

I would be remiss if I did not point out the leader of the Green Bay Packers who creates the environment for others to be successful. This kind of leader is essential for the success of the organization. The leader I am referring to is the president and CEO of the Packers, Mark Murphy. Football fans may remember Mark as an outstanding safety for the 1977–1985 Washington Redskins. Mark led the NFL in interceptions with nine in '83 and was named All-Pro the same year. Mark helped the Redskins win Superbowl XVII at the end of the 1982 season. He was voted the top 70 Redskin players of all time. He played under another great leader in Coach Joe Gibbs. Mark was not only a successful NFL football player but acquired his MBA degree from American University's Kogod School of Business while playing for the Redskins. Mark also accomplished his JD degree from the Georgetown University Law Center in 1988. Upon completion of his law degree, Mark worked as a trial attorney for the U.S. Department of Justice from 1988 until 1992. Mark increased his managerial skills as athletic director for his alma mater, Colgate, and later at Northwestern University. He was voted Packers president on December 3, 2007. The Packers won Superbowl XLV in the 2010 season, giving him his second Superbowl accomplishment and first Superbowl as an executive, in a storied career. To my knowledge, this makes Mark Murphy the first person to win a Superbowl as a player and an executive. You can read more about him on Wikipedia. I respectfully call him "Murph" as athletes often call their friends and those they like by their nickname. Mark is proof that leaders are readers. He is also proof that leaders are great people who care about others around them. He has been married forty-two years to his lovely wife, Laurie, which is another sign of his goodness. He has bolstered the Packers organization by developing the area around Lambeau field with the Titletown project, and specifically the association with the Microsoft Corporation. This development will not only increase value and revenue to the organization but should assist the Packers with winning the vote to host the NFL draft in Green Bay, I am hoping. If you ever could correspond with Murph, you will understand exactly what I am referring to about his intelligence, respect for others, success, and kindness. Murph is a leader and a person I would encourage other leaders to emulate. I greatly respect him.

Tony Dungy is another example of an excellent coach and leader who cares. Coach Dungy began his NFL coaching career in Pittsburgh as a young assistant coach and later became the head coach of the Indianapolis Colts. With the Colts and Peyton Manning, he also marked grounds as the first African American coach to win a Super Bowl on February 4, 2007. To this day, Coach Dungy is one of the softest-spoken and most polite coaches you will ever meet. He is known for treating his players with his Christian values. I enjoy listening to his perspective as an NFL television announcer before, during, and after games. Although Coach Dungy may not lead like other coaches, he, by no mistake, is a great leader. Coach Dungy is the kind of man I would have enjoyed playing for or coaching with in my lifetime. Coach Tony Dungy is a leader and a person I would encourage other leaders to emulate.

The last coach I love to watch is Coach Bill Belichick. I do not know him as a person, but I have and still strictly watch and read about his leadership as a football coach. He has led the New England Patriots to four Super Bowls in sixteen years, which is a rare accomplishment in the NFL. Alone, coaching the same team for sixteen years is remarkable. I would bet Coach Belichick uses many of the concepts I have touched on in this book to lead his team. It only makes sense that he must hire talented people to help him and train them properly. He must graduate their workload or promote them as they grow. He must communicate very clearly and very well. He must mentor them underneath his responsibility, which include players and coaches. I would bet Coach Belichick would even tell you how the team's owner, Robert Kraft, has mentored him on certain aspects of leadership. I have watched interviews with his players in which they explain how Coach Belichick teaches that the team comes first. When the team wins, the individual accomplishments and recognition will ensue. From his successes, interviews, and reviews from players and coaches alike, I can tell Coach Belichick gets the point: it is about more than you.

Another great leader I have encountered in my life is Dr. James Zaenglein, a professor at Northern Michigan University and one of my favorite teachers/professors. In his marketing strategy course, I remember Dr. Z, as we called him, telling the class the best salesperson is not always the best sales manager. When I first heard this idea, my mind was stumped because it did not make sense. Surely, if a person was the best, then no one else could be better at showing others how to be number 1 than the person who was number 1.

Dr. Z went on to explain to the class why his statement was true. He explained the best salesperson often has natural talent and can learn how to adapt to any situation. This person can learn over time how to think on their feet and close a sale. However, this person also tends to want to remain number 1; thus, they do not often like sharing their information and often hold back on little or small concepts that may make a big difference in the success of a sale. Dr. Z said the best manager is the person who is a good salesperson and enjoys showing others how to be successful.

As I gained experience in both the management and marketing sectors of business after college, I found that Dr. Z was 100 percent right. When I worked in management, where I ran the top operations, people asked me many questions about how I did so or what secrets I could share with them. I would give them a blueprint I used and was happy to think I could help them. During a conference call once, one of my upper-level managers told me to share some things but not to tell them all our secrets. This manager proves Dr. Z's point.

After my eleven-year management career, I began a career in pharmaceutical sales. Again, I found that many successful sales reps did not want to share too much of their knowledge with me. They would give me a little piece of advice here or there but would not tell me further details. As an example, they would not share details that were important to know to schedule meetings and make sales, such as who the key player was at the front of a doctor's office to get me access to the doctor(s) or schedule appointments. The best salespeople do not want to take the time to train others or give up their secrets. Therefore, the reason these people are not the best managers is because they do not want to train, help, or take the time to aid another person's improvement. When you find a salesperson who is both number 1 in sales and wants to train others, you have found a rare diamond. In your business, I hope you will recognize a prospective hire who exhibits this rare combination and find ways to retain them in your company.

Lastly, leaders are not afraid to fail. Leaders start from a point of failure. Leaders know they do not think like everyone else. They often think or know what is right to do, but others do not understand them. People will often tell them how they are wrong or that their way of thinking and/or ideas do not make sense. On the other end, leaders often are subjected to this negativity, rejection, and remarks from others that they should follow the norm and lose their innovative ideas. The successes I have shared with you thus far were still obtained, although others did not agree with me until I proved it.

Here is a list of several well-known leaders who overcame failures to achieve great success:

- Amelia Earhart
- Nikola Tesla
- Will Smith
- Albert Einstein
- Charles Smith
- James Brown
- General Patton
- Mother Teresa
- Mahatma Gandhi
- Barbara Walters
- Oprah Winfrey

- King David
- Dr. Martin Luther King
- Muhammad Ali
- Eminem
- Denzel Washington
- Sojourner Truth
- My favorite: Jesus of Nazareth (My Lord and My God)

This is not an all-inclusive list. I simply wanted to share some amazing people in history who were not afraid to be judged as a failure. These leaders had a great vision, they knew who they were, they knew the right thing to do, and they did not let others change them from being who they were.

Leaders are like a tide of water; they make *all* ships floating on its surface rise higher together.

I love leaders for many reasons, more than just because they can give confidence to others and make the world a better place. Mostly, I love how they make this world and the next limitless. They remind us the only limit we have is the power we assign to our imagination and faith.

I was told "he" was coming into the building. The "he" I'm referring to was the division manager, Bob. I was told by my manager to have my tie on, look sharp, make sure the building was clean with no parcels on the floor, and not talk too much. I was fine with all these instructions; did he have to put the last one in there? I was told Bob was an angry manager. I was told he was young and cocky and did not accept any excuses. I was fine with this since I did not plan on offering any. I remember my mind wandering during the operation and imagining what "he" looked like. Would he really want to vent his anger on me? I just started with the company a day earlier.

He came in as my team was wrapping up their jobs. He was very professional and young looking, compared to my direct manager. He was dressed in a three-piece suit, and his tie was fancy and tied perfectly. His thick hair was combed and jelled. His shoes shone as if they just came out of the box. He walked briskly from office to office. I knew I was going to like this person. He came across as organized and knowledgeable. My manager introduced me to him, "This is Bob Crouch, our division manager." He smiled, shook my hand, and welcomed me to the company and his team. He asked me how I was doing so far. I told him I had a lot to learn. He laughed and told me, "Remember one thing, there is nothing in this company you cannot learn. Our methods are made up from people who learned how to perform the job the best way, and if I can learn it, anyone could learn it." I appreciated Bob's encouragement and explanation. Funny, he did not seem like an angry person to me.

I remember telling a friend over the phone, who worked in another part of the state for our company, how Bob seemed to be really organized. My friend told me that Bob is so organized, it has been said that he has a file for his hair comb in his desk. This comment made me laugh aloud or "LOL" if we're "text talking." In 1987, there were no "LOLs," "BRBs," or "TTYLs." Bob and I became friends quickly. I asked Bob questions, and he returned solid advice. I implemented his advice and used my people skills to cement his ideas. I became successful, which made Bob successful, due to his support. We only worked together for five months, and Bob told me he was losing me because I received a promotion, which would require relocation. I told him to tell the person who wanted to move me, the answer was no. He informed me he was the person who wanted to move me. He informed his manager, who happened to run all of Michigan, except Metro Detroit, how I was ready for a full-time supervision position. He told me how the company liked when management people were not afraid to relocate because it helped the company grow and make room for more good people. I told him I really liked working with him, but he assured me this move was beneficial to both my career and the company. He informed me how others had big plans for me and said, "Besides, we may get the chance to work together again, and you can call me anytime." This comment gave me a confident feeling. It made me more relaxed in hopes I would have Bob as my manager again in the future. Bob was not just a manager who robotically said, "The company comes first." He lived this statement. He lived for his job to spot and attract talented people to hire within the company. After this, he lived for his job to train new hires well and move them up or over so they could help the company. He did not try to hold me back, even when I wanted him to. Bob was a leader. He cared about the customer, the company, and others. He did not let his own desires come before the good of the company. From day one when I nervously anticipated meeting Bob for the first time, before he even spoke, his appearance told me he was a leader. However, I was to find out later, not all leaders look this professional.

My next manager was Randy Rand, who also became one of my favorite managers and mentors. Randy was professional like Bob. He was dressed very sharp and had a clean haircut. He looked like a highway patrol officer. Randy was funny, intelligent, and caring; and like Bob, he wanted to train others and get out of their way to allow them to grow. Randy taught me everything I knew about safety in the company. He helped me obtain success in operations by showing me how everything starts with safety and caring. Randy is the reason I became successful as a district safety supervisor for the company. Randy, also like Bob, was very complimentary of my personality, work ethic, and people skills. I wrote another book about attitudes like Bob and Randy have and the power they carry. Randy and Bob are mentioned in that book because they live the success the book is referring. Today, our families and we are still friends. In fact, I wish every manager in every company were a Randy, Steven, or Bob.

Three years later, I had another great manager (Steven Thompson whom I mentioned before), but one whose appearance differed from Randy's and Bob's. As the corporate automation's manager, he oversaw the R&D team for the company, but I did not know this when I met him. Once a week, he would leave early to travel from our work location to another part of the state to finish his doctorate degree. While I was under his assignment, he completed this degree, so I told him how impressed I was with this accomplishment. He smiled and thanked me. He was a more relaxed, older, and seemingly quiet man. He listened very well to others, especially during our weekly Monday morning meetings. I felt like Steven was like a good father put in charge of our company to mentor its "children" to become creative, insightful, caring, intelligent, detail-oriented, and thoughtful leaders.

He is the reason I was able to spend time analyzing equipment in order to come up with an answer to improve the process. He believed in me and made me feel like I could accomplish anything. I really loved working with Steven. He could see our individual strengths and would point them out to us individually and in front of our group. Steven was a master at complimenting people on their strengths. He was just as good as a leader as Bob and Randy; it just took a bit longer to notice. Steven had a more subdued presence and carried himself with a quiet confidence. To emphasize my admiration for Bob, Randy, and Steven, I would take the offer to work for any of these men over an offer from another company for more money. These men were leaders who cared. They took their jobs seriously but did not take themselves too seriously and knew how to subdue their egos. They focused on mentoring less experienced managers to make the company better. They wanted results, but they did not let their ego stand in the way of allowing others to also succeed. They did not take the credit for themselves but gave the credit to those they mentored. These three men were intelligent, funny, kind, organized, detailed, professional in dress and behavior, and, most importantly, caring. In short, they are examples of excellent leaders.

Leaders do not always have to wear suits or look like a million dollars on the outside. Today, more than ever, computer programmers who work in less formal clothes have allowed the office worker to dress more casually. I personally like this fact. I like to wear a more relaxed polo shirt and dress pants to work instead of a suit. Besides, it is less expensive on the personal budget. I do like to dress in a suit for larger, more significant meetings and when interacting with customers.

I have found that work attire differs in various regions of the country. When I lived and worked in the Midwest, I thought everyone wore a suit to work. Today, I live in Florida. Many of those in the business world, with obvious exceptions like funeral homes or attorney offices, commonly wear polo shirts and khakis.

Therefore, if we cannot spot a leader by their clothes, how do we spot them? Through my experience, I have realized the answer to this question: by their interactions. A leader is caring, primarily.

They take time to mentor others. They will stop and talk to others who have questions. I recall my former spouse winning a raffle for my son, and the prize was an invitation to an Orlando Magic vs. Detroit Pistons basketball scrimmage. The game was held at the Van Andel Arena in Grand Rapids, Michigan, where we lived. Prior to the scrimmage, the winners were invited with one guest (my son chose me) to eat dinner with two Pistons players at the arena. After we had a great catered meal, the event coordinator gave us instructions for a contest that would be held during the scrimmage. My son and his competitor, another boy his age, started at the end court line during the first timeout. They had to run to the free throw line and put on a pair of NBA-size shoes, then run to the half-court line and put on an NBA-size jersey, then grab the basketball, run to the opposite free throw line while dribbling the ball, and make a basket. The first one to make it won a $50 certificate. My son, Thomas Anthony, and I were excited for this fun contest. Just as we were walking out of the room, an incredibly special guest appeared and greeted us. It was Mr. Richard DeVos, the founding owner of Amway Corporation and the owner of the Orlando Magic team.

Mr. DeVos said hi to us and asked us if we were having fun. We told him how excited we were and that Thomas was thrilled to take pictures with the two Detroit Pistons players. I explained to my son who Mr. DeVos was so he could understand his importance and thank him, which he did. Mr. DeVos grew a big smile on his face and told him he was most welcome. He told my son how polite he was for a young man and asked my son how old he was. Thomas answered, "Nine." At this time, Mr. DeVos's assistant reminded him that he had to be somewhere in five minutes. Mr. DeVos acknowledged her and went back to speaking with young Thomas. He asked him if he was excited to be on the floor with the players. Thomas assured him he was excited and a little nervous. Mr. DeVos reassured him he was going to do great. Again, his assistant tried to keep him on schedule and told him he had three minutes to be at his next appointment. Mr. DeVos kindly put up his pointer finger in a manner to say, "One minute." He asked Thomas if he played basketball at home or school along with a few other questions. He treated my son as if he were the most important person in the arena. My son and I have never forgotten this kindness from such a great leader.

Mr. DeVos was more successful in business than most. His personal net worth was aired on the local radio every year; one year, it was stated at $4 billion. After I witnessed the way he treated my son, I proclaimed, "Yes, and he's worth every penny of it." There were no cameras or reporters around when he spoke with my son. This shows a lot about the kind of person Mr. DeVos is—he genuinely cares about people. He has invested a lot of money into the local, state, and country's economy. He also has invested time with people because leaders know how important this is. I pray God continues to bless Mr. DeVos and his family.

Sometimes a leader will give a clear answer, while other times, they may challenge the person they are mentoring or training to come up with the answer on his or her own. They will make the person feel comfortable with coming to them with the perceived correct answer.

Leaders will compliment others who work with them. They understand the power of the compliment. They understand how this power fuels an employee to move forward.

Leaders are deeply knowledgeable in their area of responsibility. They study, listen, ask others who know questions they may not, and learn every detail of whatever entity, whether it be a business, person, or relationship, to make it successful. They are lifelong learners who appear to have an insatiable desire for knowledge and improvement. Leaders, whom I have come to know, enjoy teaching others how to be successful. They enjoy mentoring and helping their companies and others. Leaders tend to encourage others to be themselves and recognize the uniqueness of each person attempting to learn more. I have never heard a mentor or leader of mine tell me to be like them. They often told me I could become better than they were at something or they wish they had my characteristics in some way. I felt and still feel they could perform a task or leadership better than I could, but they never said this about themselves.

Leaders also do not fear failure. They understand what it takes to be successful. Often, they experience failure and are reminded of it by others but then eventually prove those people wrong and succeed.

I was once told by my manager when I was a part-time supervisor how it would take me two years before I may or may not be asked to join the company full-time. I knew that I worked well with my team and that I would be promoted before one year. Well, I cannot say I knew 100 percent, but I had a good idea. I also realized that failure was the alternative route, but this never concerned me. I knew that by praying, treating my employees properly, inspiring them to be number 1, and rewarding the good employees, we would be successful. I was asked to join the company full-time after seven months. Again, I give all credit to God and those nine men on my team who made me look good. I discuss how I took over a terrible, least-best operation in another chapter in the book. In this operation, I had to train my supervisors, but realized this would increase costs. If I was not successful in my idea of training them to improve the operation, it was going to kill my career. Once a person is labeled ineffective as an operator in a company, often it causes a drop in their value as a leader. I knew this, but I had no fear. Leaders know the right thing to do, and they do it. Did those supervisors deserve to be trained properly and given the tools to do their job? Absolutely, and they proved me right by showing the rest of their peers how to turn an operation around. Most employees of a company care, and leaders understand this fact. Leaders do not fear failing as much as they fear not doing what they know is right.

Leaders do not always do what is right, but they do the right thing. What do I mean? Doing what is right (in the case of me training my supervisors) would be to not train them. Remember, the division manager said he did not want me to train them but to make them do the work of the employees and I should do their job. I did not do this exactly. I did what he asked, but after the operation, I continued to train my people, as they deserved. This was doing the "right thing" in my opinion. Another example I can offer to understand this better: driving the speed limit on the highway is doing what is right, but speeding to get a person to the hospital who is having a baby or a heart attack is doing the right thing. However, I am not paying your ticket if you get one.

Leaders can be spotted by their vision. I have often found that leaders have a vision for a more successful result than those who follow them. A great example of this type of leader is Coach Jim Valvano, who coached North Carolina State men's basketball team in 1983 and brought them to an NCAA tournament championship. The players thought he was crazy on the first day he introduced himself. He told them he envisioned them winning a national championship and brought out a ladder and placed it under the hoop. He had each player climb the ladder and cut a piece of the net, as if they just won the championship and were cutting the net to take home. I recall the players telling this story and hearing the amazement in their voices.

Not only did Coach Valvano lead his team to a national championship, but his team caused one of the biggest upsets in college basketball history by winning the game. Leaders envision things others do not. They see more success for their group than the group does itself.

I recently worked as an operations manager for a construction company. My territory was the entire northeast and most of the northwest portion of Florida. I told my employees we would be the number 1 division in one year, and they awkwardly gawked at me as the players looked at Coach Valvano. As one of four satellite divisions, they asked me how we would accomplish this. I explained I would make sure they thoroughly knew how to perform their jobs by training them well. They needed to be productive, and I would work on my end to obtain more business. I would personally call customers and join associations in our industry to build relationships with potential customers. I would be more responsive to our current customers to ensure excellent, consistent service. We would count on our internal customers in the home office to obtain more business for us and complete our billing. I told them I would hire skilled people to grow our operation from two divisions to four. I would spend more time interviewing the right people and hire them to start the two divisions we needed to grow our company. I promised them I would hire others who would do their job, so my crew did not have to work harder to cover for them. This would set us apart in the minds of those in our industry, which is a one-stop shop for construction needs. I would treat my people fairly with accountability and rewards for those who achieve above average results. I told them that we would grow this company together. We will make the customers happy and help the company to monetarily grow, and we would see increased income. We accomplished this goal. We grew from nine to eighteen employees and from two to four divisions. I promoted three employees to the foremen level and hired nine additional employees. This means nine more families had bills paid and food on the table due to growing the company. We doubled revenue by 234 percent and reduced expenses by 1.7 percent compared to these numbers by the manager before me. The vision was set, and the men aspired to it. Vision is essential for leaders. Not everyone has a vision, but every leader has one.

Today, well-known business leaders include Richard Branson, Elon Musk, Bill Gates, Warren Buffett, Marissa Mayer, Mark Zuckerberg, Donald Trump, Indra Nooyi, Virginia Rometty, Ursula Burns, Zhang Xin, and Jeff Bezos. From recorded interviews and articles, they have all stated they had a vision for their company or companies. There is an old saying, "If you don't know where you're going, how are you going to get there?" These leaders knew where they wanted to go and lead others in getting there.

Leaders do not make mistakes, or do they? Leaders will often tell you of some of their greatest blunders. I once read an interview in which Mark Cuban told the interviewer a time when he was fired. Well, this is one thing I have in common with Mark. He said this was the best thing to ever happen to him. Leaders will tell you they have made mistakes, but it is important to remember a few things about these mistakes. Sometimes leaders make mistakes by being bold. They often have a large goal or vision, and when someone has a large task in front of them, there are many areas to make a mistake in. People who are not leaders think smaller, have less confidence, do not say what they are thinking, and usually are not out in front leading a group. Therefore, it is less likely they will make a mistake.

In 1928, John A. Shedd significantly stated,

> Ships in a harbor are safe, but that is not what ships are built for.

Leaders are like ships. They are not made to be safe. They take us places we cannot see until we get there. Leaders carry us along with them. They get us through the storms if we help them. When we arrive at their vision, we experience things we never imagined and learn things about ourselves. Leaders bring us to a place where we can start or build dreams.

Leaders have a passion for their vision within their company. They want the best for everyone, not just themselves. They know if the company is successful, everyone will enjoy the gains. In short, leaders care!

However, leaders are not always agreeable. There have been a few times where my manager was not happy with me. I challenged them in areas I believed, without doubt, were too important to ignore. I have encountered situations where a manager or owner thought production was more important than safety. I knew from experience that when safety is a personal value, it allows the same people to do the same job every day. In a safe environment, those people provide better service, safety, and production. I have seen that prioritizing production over the expense of safety leads to loss of both. Several owners of companies I worked for told me they do not like working with women. I responded that some of the best people I have worked with in the past have been women. I had a business owner ask me in an interview if I am hard on people. He had family members who worked for him, so he did not want me to offend them. I asked him why he wanted me to work for him. He explained they were doing well, but he knew they could do a lot better. I asked him if he felt the people in his company had become complacent. He responded yes, and he hoped that I could improve both processes and profits. I explained I would go out of my way to not offend anyone in his company. However, I explained that when I show others where to improve, this might come off as offensive without me being rude. He asked me why I thought this would happen. I told him I learned from my past that when I have improved a process or group, those who were responsible for that area were automatically offended. I call it the "mirror effect." They look at their own incompleteness and realize they could have done better. Although this business owner did not hire me, I still audited his company's website and e-mailed him several errors I found. He e-mailed me back with an appreciated "thank you." This example demonstrates that leaders do not always agree. It reminds me of a quote I have on my calendar:

> If two people in a company ALWAYS agree, one of them is not necessary.

A good leader wants honest people around. They do not fear honesty or truth. They want to improve every day and thus understand they need to accept ideas to do so. One of the most important skills leaders have is the ability to spot talent. The American philosopher Elbert Hubbard stated (1901),

> There is something that is much more scarce, something rarer than ability. It is the ability to recognize ability.

For those who have talent, I remind them talent is wasted if it is not encompassed by hard work and determination. Stay focused and determined to prevent laziness from taking over. You may find that you can accomplish goals easier than others can, but do not let this convince you to relax and offer less of yourself. Raise your goals to a higher level and bring others with you. This is about more than you are.

So how do you spot a leader? Look around you, be observant, listen, watch, and you will find a leader. You will most likely find this person helping someone else. They will dig into entry-level work alongside an employee at times. They will be sharing their knowledge, understanding, passion, and vision. This person will be taking responsibility; they will not sit back and let someone else do all the work. They will be out in front leading the charge. They will be encouraging others, motivating them to perform to the best of their ability. They will be laughing and smiling. They enjoy what they do in life and often have a great sense of humor. They will spend time training their supervisors or managers. Then they will step back and let the people they once trained become mentors of other people. Like a ship, they will be carrying others to a better place. Employees, like shipmates, will go where their captain steers them. Who is your captain?

17

Empowering Great Leaders

People ask the difference between a leader and a
boss. The leader leads, and the boss drives.
—Theodore Roosevelt

Hire good leaders and stay out of their way. Coach them when necessary, but do not micromanage them.

The following excerpt was taken from Wikipedia on May 20, 2015, which describes some trials and tribulations of Ludwig van Beethoven:

> There is no authentic record of the date of his birth; however, the registry of his baptism, in a Roman Catholic service at the Parish of St. Regius on 17 December 1770, survives. As children of that era were traditionally baptized the day after birth in the Catholic Rhine country, and it is known that Beethoven's family and his teacher Johann Albrechtsberger celebrated his birthday on 16 December, most scholars accept 16 December 1770, as Beethoven's date of birth.
>
> Beethoven had other local teachers: the court organist Gilles van den Eeden (d. 1782), Tobias Friedrich Pfeiffer (a family friend, who taught Beethoven the piano), and Franz Rovantini (a relative, who instructed him in playing the violin and viola). Beethoven's musical talent was obvious at a young age.
>
> Sometime after 1779, Beethoven began his studies with his most important teacher in Bonn, Christian Gottlob Neefe, who was appointed the Court's Organist in that year. His first three piano sonatas, named "Kurfürst" ("Elector") for their dedication to the Elector Maximilian Friedrich (1708–1784), were published in 1783. *Maximilian Frederick noticed Beethoven's talent early and subsidized and encouraged the young man's musical studies.*
>
> In March 1787, Beethoven traveled to Vienna (possibly at another's expense) for the first time, apparently in the hopes of studying with Mozart. The details of their relation-

> ship are uncertain, including whether they even actually met. Having learned his mother was ill, Beethoven returned about two weeks after his arrival. His mother died shortly thereafter, and his father lapsed deeper into alcoholism. As a result, Beethoven became responsible for the care of his two younger brothers, and spent the next five years in Bonn.
>
> …Beethoven was probably first introduced to Joseph Haydn in late 1790, when the latter was traveling to London and stopped in Bonn around Christmas time… Mozart had also recently died. Count Waldstein, in his farewell note to Beethoven, wrote: "Through uninterrupted diligence you will receive Mozart's spirit through Haydn's hands." (emphasis added)

Did you notice how Beethoven learned from each person in his life? His father was his first teacher, and then he worked with family and friends. He later aimed to work with others as his mentors to learn more. Leaders have a passion to be the best they can be. They look for mentors. Beethoven attempted to meet one of the masters of his time, Mozart, but self-sacrifice was required when his mother became ill and passed.

The idea of self-sacrifice is another quality a leader demonstrates. I mentioned earlier how a leader will give up an ascending manager for the good of the company and each individual.

From the above excerpt, did you notice how Beethoven took care of his two younger brothers after his mother passed, since his father was unable to? Leaders help and care for others. They know life is about more than their success. They understand their happiness comes from helping others and seeing others succeeds, as well as themselves.

How can we empower great leaders? Before encountering or working with a leader, we must spot them. It was mentioned how several people observed Beethoven's talent and passed him on to a more talented teacher after working with or mentoring him. I believe we should do the same with leaders in a company—pass them on to others who can further mentor them.

Cross-training in different departments to gain knowledge of the inner workings of the company creates a great understanding. A great understanding leads to solid decision-making. UPS is excellent at this practice, and their success is no mistake.

I started my career as an industrial engineer, but remember, I was a marketing management major in college. Why would a company place me in the engineering department? You talk about a fish out of water. Did they think I was going to help this portion of the company? No, they did not, not right away. This company knew I would be a much better operations manager if I knew and believed in the company's time/motion studies. The leaders of this company were 100 percent correct, and I applaud their wise decision. I became a much better leader and operations manager due to this cross-training. I was later trained in three different operations: HR, R&D, and training. I also led workshops and traveled about the state troubleshooting. It is no mistake that this company leads their industry by far. They are called UPS, and "Service is their last name."

Leaders must keep an open mind.

I shared this idea and method of cross-training with an owner of a construction company. He said the idea was too costly, and he did not want to implement such practice. Yet he constantly complained about managers and others not completing an item needed by another department. He often complained how some leaders did not have the skills they needed to make the company better. Leaders must keep an open mind if they are to succeed and help the company succeed. An open mind would have allowed this owner to see certain concepts as an investment instead of a cost.

Remember, the rate of the leader determines the pace of the pack.

If the leader keeps an open mind and strives to implement ideas, which are proven to work by great companies, the people in the company will do the same. The result will be success.

Next, we need to train leaders to establish a stronger foundation. Beethoven was trained by more accomplished artists of his time. Therefore, the principle of primacy and training an employee correctly from the start is so critical.

We need to provide leaders with ideas, books, computer programs, other people, and our own vision of how great they can be, without limiting them. Companies should provide them with reports of the operations or departments they lead. This will allow them to pinpoint the areas that are successful and those that need attention. As I mentioned earlier, leaders have an insatiable desire to learn and grow. I know I do. Challenge leaders to envision success or a goal beyond their knowledge, which will enhance their imagination. Our imagination is only limited by our dreams of what is possible. Challenge them to dream bigger and more boldly, without limitations. Coach Tom Izzo (Michigan State Basketball) has always signed all autographs with "Dream Big." Einstein reflected that *imagination is more important than knowledge*. Why do you think this is?

Next, we can listen to leaders and become better for it. Beethoven's audience was sometimes simple bystanders who simply enjoyed his talent, and other times it was his mentor. Leaders need to be listened to for us to see how they are progressing and taking us with them in their vision. They may have to be fine-tuned here or there by a mentor, but we will notice how the leader is growing in their abilities and taking us further into their journey, a place we are unable to go alone. Listening to a leader is like music to our ears, and in Beethoven's case, it was music. It allows us to offer feedback via applause or some other form of appreciation. This feedback fuels the leader to keep going, feel supported, and have assurance that they are on the correct path.

Years ago, while I was still in college and working my first job, I ran into a problem needing a solution, which is something we will all encounter in our first jobs. A veteran driver approached me and complained that one of my loaders was not loading his truck properly. I asked more questions to better understand the issue to determine if I could solve the problem. After listening to the driver describe how he delivered his route, I realized I had no idea what he was experiencing.

I did not understand why it mattered that one package had to be ahead of another just because of the direction he was driving down a road. Why couldn't he just park and run across the road? He kept saying it cost him too much time to sort the shelf full of packages, which were out of place. I finally decided to go on his route with him and see for myself. I asked my manager, Jack (not his real name), if I could do this; but he said it was against company policy to let part-time supervisors out on the trucks. I did not stop there. I then asked my division manager, Bob, if he could give me permission to do ride with the driver. He also agreed it was against company policy but encouraged me to call the HR department head, Meredith, and find out why. Therefore, I did, and she explained it was due to insurance costs. I respectfully explained the issue I had with the driver and loader and how much I wanted to fix the problem. She then called the insurance company and eventually approved me to ride with the driver for just one day. This helped me understand the driver and determine a way to load his truck the right way to save him and the company time and money. I worked with the loader to better explain why each package had to be loaded a certain way. The result was the driver and the loader both thanked me for taking the extra time and effort to fix the issue. I was not only able to fix the problem but build trust and rapport with both employees. Due to the success of my operation after this ride, it became a procedure for all the operations in the state for our company. This is what leaders do. They break down barriers, improve processes, and build rapport with fellow employees.

    Support is a key and necessary step in building or standing by a leader, as they will experience career or personal hardships along the way. Beethoven experienced both when his mother passed. Professionally, it prevented him from meeting and learning from Mozart. Personally, he lost his mother and, in essence, his father and had to care for his two younger brothers. Imagine if he did not have anyone to support him during these difficult times. Two great results occur when we support a leader. One, the leader learns how others care and what that care feels like. Second, it offers them instruction on how to care for those under their leadership.

This recalls a great story I heard about CEO Jack Welch. As the leader of General Electric (GE) from 1981 to 2001, Jack grew the company by 4,000 percent in those twenty years. I do not respect Jack only because he grew GE by an astonishing amount, but also for his humbleness to share this story (excerpt from Wikipedia.com):

> I asked Jack Welch, at the World Business Forum 2011, to talk about tipping points in his life and he said, "I blew up a (GE) factory the first year I was there." He was in his mid-twenties and figured his career was over. "I was running a little pilot plant. It all exploded, went to hell." (Pilot plant refers to testing. He experimented with a new formula and KaBoom.)
>
> He went on to say, "I was called to New York because my boss didn't know me anymore once I had that accident. So he sent me to New York to explain it to the higher-ups. I was thinking I was going to get fired. He called me in the room and asked me what did you do wrong. What have you learned?"
>
> At this point, Jack's tone and eyebrows rose. "He took the Socratic Method with me and did an incredible job of engaging me in learning about what I did wrong in the process. And I learned never kick anybody when they're down. No one would ever say that I was soft by any means. But they would never say that I beat on anybody when they were down." Finally, Jack added, "Tipping points (are) learning experiences from complete failures."

How do you not love a person like Jack Welch? He is a great example of what a leader is and does. If I am ever blessed enough to meet Mr. Welch, I am going to give him a kind bear hug and thank him. His actions are exactly what I believe in. He proved what I feel is the right way to lead. Although I have never read anything about Jack Welch, I realized how much my work style is like his after hearing a couple of stories about him after I finished this book. I am shocked and honored to know I think similarly like Jack Welch from a work perspective. He is a great man and leader.

Companies are made up of people who understand that care follows a full 360° circle, where when they care for their leaders, their leaders will care for them. It is vital for a leader to remember how they cannot accomplish anything worthwhile without caring for his or her people. Leaders lead the way.

We must assist our leaders. Beethoven personally needed assistance when he had to care for his younger siblings. He professionally and financially needed assistance to travel to meet Mozart. We need to look and listen in order to understand what our leaders need help with and determine a way to assist them. We need to understand what their strength is and how to keep them focused on their task. We must assist them to eliminate things that may prevent them from doing what they do best.

A great quote from a great man, George Washington Carver:

> Since new developments are the products of a creative mind, we must therefore stimulate and encourage that type of mind in every way possible.

Mr. Carver created 518 new products and processes. He is a man I could and will read about for years to come. He was a gift from God without doubt.

We must show appreciation for leaders. Appreciation via words and deeds is what shows a leader that they are doing great things and to keep going. The appreciation is the compliment we offer in action and words, which propels the leader forward. Encouragement is like training—it should never end. Imagine knowing that the moment you walk through the door into work every day, you are going to be cheered by applauding employees, managers, and leaders. Who would not want this every day? Leaders need to be appreciated, trained, if needed, and encouraged. Who would not want to come to work in this fashion?

Lastly, let them be leaders. It is who they are, and it is what they do. Another great quote by Lee Iacocca:

> I hire people brighter than me and then I get out of their way.

I think this is a great recipe for dealing with leaders when they are hitting their stride. When we get in the way of great leaders, it is like stopping Beethoven during a concerto; you can only make it worse. Allow a leader to flow into the zone where they know what is needed next and they are feeling what they are doing. Like a great composer, leaders have a flow and magic all their own. The best we can do is limiting them when necessary, while the worst we can do is cause them to stop their flow and walk off. Let leaders be leaders. You will love the sound of the company music if you do.

Lastly, protect yourself as an insurance that your company will not suffer if a leader does leave the company. This reminds me of what a former HR manager said to me when discussing an employee who requested a day off, "What would you do if they died or were injured and in the hospital?" I replied I would have to find a way to replace them. He replied, "Then do it when they need you to."

The leader of your company may not leave due to their will. What can you do to make sure you do not injure the company by losing too much money or customers due to this unforeseen event? The "key person" policy is one great tool companies and leaders implement to protect their company.

Before I explain how to protect your company by using this policy, let me remind you to check with your insurance agent on all local, state, and federal laws regarding this form of protection. Also, check with your attorney to ensure that you comply with all laws. The state where I sold these life insurance plans made it legal to do so. But I cannot speak for all states or new laws that may arise. Call your insurance agent yourself to double-check.

The policy was initially called a "key man" policy. Today, we call it a "key person" policy because so many great leaders are women. A "key person" is someone who leads the company in some capacity to the degree in which if they were no longer in the company, it would suffer greatly. Losing this person would cause a significant drop in production, service, and/or safety. In other words, you would lose a significant amount of revenue and profit from the loss of their leadership and knowledge.

So how do you protect yourself or the business from this hit or loss of revenue? You talk to your insurance agent, if they have not approached you already, and you take out a "key person" policy. Also, take out a life insurance policy on this employee, which reads if this person dies, the policy pays out the agreed premium to you, the business owner. The amount of this premium will be determined by yourself and your insurance agent based on how much revenue you believe would be lost in their absence. The first question you must ask is "How long would it take me to replace them or their income, which they generated?" The second question is "What would it cost me to go out and hire this person immediately?" These two questions will give you a decent idea of how much your policy or replacement value should be on this "key person."

It also helps them feel more appreciated by your company. I have had friends and family say how they would miss their Christmas bonus if they left a company to join another. This is one reason they do not look around for a better opportunity. Who does not enjoy a $1,000, $5,000, or $10,000 bonus each year? If you interview for a leadership position, you will find that executive managers ask about the bonus program in many companies. Remember, leaders have a vision of where they want the company to grow. They know they need solid leaders to get the company to its goal. Once you find these great leaders, you do not want to lose them to the competition. This "key person" policy also ensures your succession plan.

Lastly, do not forget about yourself. I have sat down with several wealthy business owners to discuss their succession plan. The first question I ask, which usually results in a blank look, is "When are you going to die?" The business owner has worked their tail off for years, and they have done most things well, which is why they are still in business. However, remember the key word is *worked*, as in they *worked* their tail off. This means they often kept their nose to the grindstone. They were too busy growing and keeping up with the growth to stop and think about future events with logic and well-thought-out ideas. I then ask them, "What amount do you think you could sell your business?" After they respond, I further question, "What amount do you think you would get if you passed away?" Many business owners have never considered this idea. I also ask them who would buy the business. Sometimes they know exactly who would buy it, whether it is a family member or a current employee. The next question I ask, which turns their smile upside down, is "Do you realize when you pass, your spouse or children, unless they are very knowledgeable in the business, will be offered pennies on the dollar for your company?" This is just the way the market works. If a spouse or surviving members of the business owner have been involved in the business and are very competent, the buyer knows they can run the company. Therefore, in order to buy the company, the buyer must give a closer to market value of the business worth.

However, if the buyer knows the spouse or other family members do not know how to sustain the business, they will offer a low-ball value and usually get it. The purchaser knows their competition. They know if the surviving family members do not want the headache; they will take advantage. If the buyer knows the company will lose money due to their incompetence, they will bring this up in negotiating the price of the purchase. They will remind the surviving family members that they can get more for it now compared to when the books show a great loss of revenue and profit. The family members will usually agree since they don't know or want the business. When I walk through this with the business owner, their eyes open, but their smile quickly turns into a frown. I go on to further explain if the purchaser is a "key person," they know what would happen to the company if the surviving family attempts to run it. Therefore, they will purchase it for less. According to televised mafia (a.k.a. *The Sopranos* and *The Godfather*), "it's not personal, it's business."

Therefore, do not just make a succession plan in place with a "key person" policy or policies, but have it written and documented in a contract. This locks in the agreement and makes it legal. This will allow you, the business owner, to get the maximum value for your company. If you pass away, it will provide a true value to your family. You must protect yourself. You are a leader. Leaders, in my opinion, deserve more because they risk more. If you want more, know that reward does not come without risk.

18

Group Leaders

Everyone ought to be prepared to take the helm.
—Henrik Johan Ibsen

Scott, a PT supervisor, approached me one day and asked me how I became a manager at such a young age. I explained that I had great mentors who helped me understand the company and that I did what they showed me or told me to do. I studied the methods, procedures, and policies at home when my kids went to bed. I became a knowledgeable leader of my team. When he asked me if I would mentor him, I declined. Because I was mentoring Mark, Scott's supervisor, at that time, Mark should be the one to mentor him. Scott asked me why I preferred this method. I explained how Mark would miss the opportunity to train and mentor a great group leader like Scott. It robbed Mark of the chance to grow as both a mentee and a supervisor. Besides, I thought Mark and Scott would grow closer since they had to work together every day in the same work area, whereas I only saw Scott occasionally during the shift. I also explained to Scott how it could and should create a better chemistry in the work area. Lastly, I explained to him if I became his mentor, it could backfire on him by creating animosity toward him from his group since I was the manager and it would appear I was showing favoritism. I assured Scott that Mark would be excited to mentor him, and I could not wait to see how quickly they both learn together.

Group leaders are essential to a work group for several reasons. As current and future leaders of the company, they can often lead, or shape, the attitude of the employees in the work area. Group leaders are also a great resource for employees when the supervisor or manager is not present. They can answer simple questions asked by an employee, which allows the supervisor or manager to handle concerns that are more serious. Group leaders can follow-up train a new employee, provided they have been qualified to do so by the trainer. Again, I caution the supervisor or trainer to follow up with the employee afterward and ask them what, where, why, when, and how they were trained. This is not due to a lack of trust for the group leader but rather reinsures the importance of proper and consistent training. It is also the only way to know if the trainee fully understood the training.

Group leaders are an outward sign of how a company is growing and preparing the next person to lead. This position can be a motivator to an employee who has desire to become a leader within the organization. This process reduces the "us vs. them" mentality, which sometimes occurs in certain environments between employees and their supervisors or managers.

An employee who expresses how they wish to become a group leader becomes a mentee once they establish this mindset. Training is never over, and success should be ongoing at every level in an organization. If a company does not train every day, it is not growing properly. If it is not growing properly, it is dying. Remember, your competition is reading this book, and others of its kind, to gain an edge on you. If you are not doing this, they will gladly do it and outwork you to gain or even take your customers. The company that gains and takes care of its customers best also gains in profits. You do not want prosperity? If you do not have or assign group leaders, start using them. If you use them, but you do not train them daily, start training daily. Remember, group leaders are the future of your company. How are you training for your future?

19

Mentoring

> Try Not. Do or do not. There is no try.
>
> —Yoda

My first memory of Coach Glen Brown was when I was seven years old in 1971. Later, he became one of my favorite coaches because he treated me so well. It is no wonder to me why he was such a successful coach. He was great at respecting and treating everyone with kindness and caring. I was walking toward the Hedgecock Field House on the NMU campus to attend my first-ever Northern Michigan University Wildcats men's basketball game in my hometown of Marquette, Michigan. I was unsure, excited, and surprised at the number of people entering the building.

    I was elated by the band music in the stands, the cheers of our fans, and the persisting energy buzz. All of this I could hear as I neared the door. The smell of popcorn waffled through the air as I entered the field house. I remember seeing the ushers wearing gold nylon jackets, holding the people back with their arms, and asking people to wait until the players took the floor since they were coming toward the gymnasium. I was standing just inside of the main door entrance. I was caught off guard by seeing the players coming out of the lower level via the staircase. I did not know where the players originated from since this was my first game in attendance. I remember the eye-catching look of the green, gold, and white uniform warm-ups the players wore. I recall being amazed by the height of the players—I had never seen people this tall before. I came from an Italian family where the tallest person was 5'9". Some of these players were over 6'9". I remember hearing the crowd scream as the players made their way through the gym doorway and onto the floor. The noise was so spontaneous and loud, I thought I missed a play until I realized they could not be playing since the players just passed me, but it was just fans screaming for our team. Man, I could not wait to get in the gym. I was wearing a T-shirt that had a face sketching of a Golden Wildcat on the front. This shirt also came with free entry to any NMU sporting event. My mom worked at the university's bookstore. She explained to my two brothers and me how the university offered the employees a shirt for a set amount of money. Man, I thought I died and went to heaven. I knew my parents did not have a lot of money. My mom bought those shirts knowing how much my brothers and I loved sports and would enjoy all the games in person. When I realized the love given in the shirt, how the shirt represented my college team, and how our fans screamed for our team, I floated into that gym without touching the floor. I looked to my left and could not believe how high the stands extended and how many people packed them. I was walking toward the cheerleaders at the court's end, thinking they must see the game, so I would be able to see it from where they were too. Hey, I was there to cheer also.

After I stood there watching the players warm up, an usher told me I would have to find a seat. There were so many people; I had no idea where to go. I asked the usher where to sit, but he told me to just squeeze in somewhere, and the top of the bleachers would be my best chance.

I was more than familiar with Hedgecock Field House and had attended many games there from the time I was seven years old until I left the town after graduating college at age twenty-two. I also practiced in the gym during those same youthful years. One day when I was in the fourth grade, Coach Brown came into the gym. There were many college students shooting hoops for fun and then myself. Coach Brown told everyone they had to leave since the varsity team was getting ready to practice. He growled my name, "Tommy, come here." I was worried I made a mad face or something and was in trouble. He told me to sit over on the first bleacher because he wanted to talk to me. I noticed he was not following me over to this seat. Once all the college students left the gym, he came over to me with a big smile and asked, "You really love basketball, don't you?" I assured him I did. He smiled and told me I could stay in the gym and play at a basket in the corner while he held practice. The only request he made was for me to stop dribbling if I heard him yelling. I gave him a big smile, shook his hand, thanked him, and ran off to shoot baskets. Coach Brown was a great coach, mentor, and person. Years later, one of his players, Tom Izzo, became his assistant coach and mentee. Coach Izzo went on to achieve one of the most successful careers in NCAA men's basketball history at Michigan State University, where he is still coaching well today.

Did Coach Brown know that Tom Izzo would become such an excellent coach when he was a player? I do not know for sure, but I'm guessing he did. Did he know how good of a player Tom was and how he coached the team on the court from the point guard position when Tom played? I know he did. I think by the time Tom was a junior player, Coach Brown knew he had a future assistant coach for his staff. I know Coach Brown mentored Tom when he saw that Tom wanted to be a leader. He mentored him as a player first, then as a coach when Tom finished playing.

A mentor observes willingness and uniqueness in the mentee, and if they are willing and driven to become a leader, the mentor is happy to coach them. If the mentee shows uniqueness in listening and applying what the mentor teaches them, this encourages the mentor to offer as much help as possible to enhance this person as a future leader.

Mentoring is offered to someone who has the right attitude, desire, and ability to learn. Tom Izzo had and still has a great attitude. He had the desire to play, win, and coach others. He had the ability, which was apparent to Coach Brown during Tom's years as a player, to be a leader of his team. He also knew Tom possessed a key ingredient: the desire to help others. Other players on Tom's teams may have had a good attitude or the ability to learn, but they did not have the desire to become a basketball coach and lead others in this area. Coach Tom Izzo still treats me the same great way he did when I was younger, and he was less known. He is exemplary, a great person, hard worker, and amazing mentor to his staff and players. I discuss more details and stories about Coach Izzo in another book I'm writing.

> When the Student is ready, the Teacher will appear. (Buddhist proverb)

Coach Brown witnessed that Tom Izzo was ready to take the next step in basketball and become a coach. Coach Brown started Coach Izzo down the road to becoming a great leader, and then Izzo was further mentored by Coach Jud Heathcote at MSU, where Izzo has been since 1995. If Coach Brown is such a good coach and leader, where did he get his mentoring? Coach Stan Albeck mentored Coach Brown initially and then went on become the coach of several ABA and NBA teams.

A mentor can offer discipline and knowledge to the future leader. It takes discipline and hard work to study, teach, lead, and expand upon what a leader already knows. When my mother was in the hospital, I ran into Tom Izzo's dad in the waiting room on the sixth floor. I walked in and was surprised to see him. I quickly said hi and asked how he was doing. I eventually told him how much I thought of him and his wife (Mrs. Izzo) based on how well Coach Tom treated me to this day. He smiled and thanked me. I also told Mr. Izzo that Tom's great work ethic was very apparent. He told me that he told Tom to be the hardest worker in basketball coaching once he got the job. He told him to arrive before others and leave after others. Coach Izzo does this daily. It takes knowledge to understand how to be successful and be able to consistently produce those successful results through mentoring. Mr. Izzo knew his advice and teachings would help his son do very well. Coach Tom Izzo is in the college basketball Hall of Fame and deserves every honor he has acquired. He's an outstanding person.

Understanding is not a tool just for the mentor; it is also for the mentee and future leader. The first thing a mentee must understand is that a mentor will need an adjustment time to learn how to best communicate and teach the mentee. The mentee must understand they may not function in the same way as the mentor, but it's pertinent the lesson be learned. As an example, the mentor may like to first use film to teach and offer a visual of a play on the court. The mentee may like to use live people on a floor and walk through the play. Both can be effective ways to teach. The mentee or future leader needs to recognize how their mentor trains and why they train in that such manner.

A good mentee is one who returns for follow-up questions in their early development. A good leader wants to learn as much as they can and recognizes their mentor's ability when they are stuck or unsure of the best way to proceed. A good person to mentor is someone whose ego is not too big to where it prevents success. I would like to make a sign like those in the Ole West: "Take guns off at the door." Only this sign one would read, "Take ego off at the door." Both guns and ego can be used for good, or they can be lethal to a life or career.

In chapter 6 on training, we talked about the importance of follow-up. The same rule holds true for a good leader. They will follow up with their mentor and attempt to master the knowledge at hand. A good leader cares about doing the right thing for their employees, the customers, and the company. Having this caring mindset will lead them back to the mentor if an idea arises that they are uncomfortable or unsure about.

Having the desire to be mentored by a good leader is the most important ingredient for a future leader or mentee. Talent, ability, success in a previous position, and likability are useless unless the mentee has the yearning to be mentored. The saying "Where there is a will, there is a way" reflects that the most important ingredient of success is desire or will. When you find a person who desires to be trained by a leader and mentor, then you must decide if they have the ability and proper attitude to be a leader. If these qualities are present, then this is the right person to mentor. This person loves what they do to help others and the company to grow. They have a passion for whatever line of work they are in, whether it is people, animals, robotics, etc.

You may be wondering if anyone can be mentored, or if most people have the desire, ability, and proper attitude to be mentored. This reminds me of a statement Coach Vince Lombardi made the first year he took over the Packers: "Gentlemen, everyone wants to be world champions, but very few are willing to work for it." When you find a mentee who has all the qualities we discussed and the desire to work to become a champion, you have a worthy person. In the words of Yoda from *Star Wars*, "Do or don't. There is no try."

Remember, you mentor a person so that one day they become the future leader of your company. This ensures that the company will be safe and continue to prosper. Yes, you know what is coming. In the words of Mr. Spock (Leonard Nimoy), "Live long and prosper." He just forgot to add, "By mentoring a leader." Then again, Spock was not a business owner.

Each department within a company should have a department head who mentors a prospective leader for the future. This is how the company grows and continues the successful execution of proven profitable practices. In addition, this mentoring can serve as a motivating factor for employees to perform well. From my experience, I have seen that a future leader will ask their mentor or another mentee what the mentee did to earn their position within the department. An employee who desires to attain a higher position in the future will emulate the mentee or future leader's behavior and practices. Would not running a business be easier if employees emulated the proper and successful practices of the leader ahead of them? Now, even the mentee has someone to mentor. One mentor/leader shapes one mentee to become a successor and leader. Then that new leader shapes a new mentee, and the cycle continues.

Another way to look at mentoring is through what the financial planners in the business world call "succession planning." Mentoring is a way to prepare an employee to one day become a leader and take over the company, or a portion of it. Remember: No successor = no future company.

20

Technology

Our future success is directly proportional to our ability to understand, adopt and integrate new technology into our work.[2]
—Sukant Ratnakar

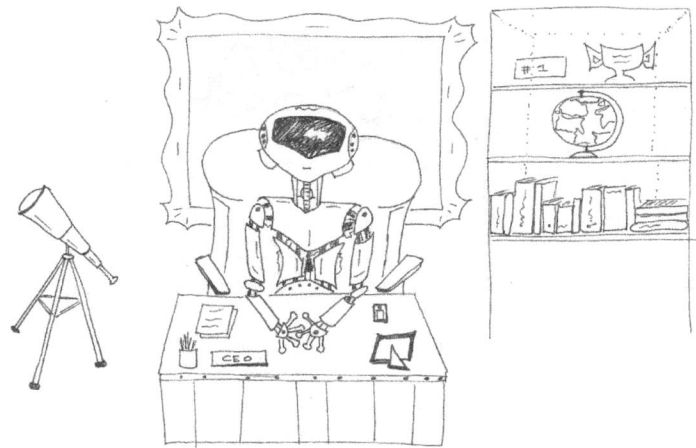

In 1978, I had the privilege of taking a class taught by an outstanding teacher, Mr. Jim Smith, in high school. I recall the day he bellowed

---

[2] https://www.quotes.mirrorreview.com/technology/quotes-on-technology-that-predict-future/

my name as I passed him standing outside of his classroom door during class change time. He was a big man at 6'4", and he had a deep voice. He used to pitch for the Chicago White Sox organization for a few years. He was known for being a great person, being a teacher, and bellowing the names of students he wanted to talk to between classes. Mr. Smith, who had been working in the computer world since the 1960s, told me computers were going to be the future and suggested I take his class. However, I found this course incredibly cumbersome and unproductive. We would punch out holes on a punch card to determine our result from the computer. We then had to place the card on a metal spool and secure it. The computer would make whining noises for several minutes and spit out our result on a black-and-white monitor. Mr. Smith was such a great person; he was funny, intelligent, and an overall great teacher. He would talk sports with me, and I appreciated his stories and humor. However, I never took another computer class again. Today, I wish I had never stopped taking those courses, as Mr. Smith was 100 percent accurate in his vision that computers are the future.

These days, technology is a critical factor in the success of any business. Specifically, computer use and automation can set a company apart from the competition. Those who understand this and tap into the potential of technology will lead their industry. Those who do not will fall behind and risk going out of business.

Computers are no longer used for just one or two departments within a company, as they were years ago when companies first began to utilize them. When I was first hired after graduating college, only three departments used computers, namely, accounting, human resources, and industrial engineering, while the others did not. Now, computers are, or should be, used throughout the entire company. They make organization, production, service, and even safety so much better.

Every leader should have reports generated automatically from computers. This reduces the amount of time a leader needs to gather critical information that provides the leader with where he or she needs to focus his or her time and energy. These reports will enable the leader to ask the appropriate questions to those working underneath him or her and find a solution if there is a problem.

Quality of products in manufacturing has increased immensely due to computer assistance. I recall an orthopedic surgeon who had a patent on back pins for spinal reconstruction of vertebrae fractures show me his manufacturing facility. He said the computerization of the pin production makes it possible to produce pin after pin that are 1/1000 of a millimeter in size. This kind of quality and speed is accomplished with minimum effort compared to manually making the pins. Automated manufacturing of these pins increases production accuracy, enhances safety, and allows the physician to perform more consistent and successful surgeries.

My son is currently studying to become a doctor of anesthesia. He will be an amazing anesthetist for several reasons. He is passionate, intelligent, and caring and learns quickly. He knows what he is doing and why he is doing it. The other major reason he will be successful is due to his understanding of technology. While attending college as an undergrad, he worked in his university's IT (information technology) department. He is capable of working on both software and hardware. I believe that a hospital or office needing a person with this kind of skill set will greatly benefit from his computer knowledge. He can fix viruses, replace hardware breakdowns, and maintain computer speed, to name a few simple fixes he is capable of. He can also design websites, program software interface, and maintain social media sites for advertisement. Another pertinent knowledge today, my son understands what certain social media sites are used for and by who runs them. He knows and understands this and remains current by communicating with his friends who also work in IT. He understands platforms in terms of which ones work best based on specific needs. I told him, jokingly, if I had his knowledge, ability, and skill, I could rule the world. He then jokingly asked why I would not work with him to learn and develop this ability—him as the mentor, me as the mentee. I precautiously explained why I did not want to rule the world.

In 1989, I worked in a company's R&D department. I was assigned to the automation of an operation, where the R&D was taking place. The automation of the equipment included motorized belts and rollers, photo eyes, cameras (which communicated with computers to move a paddle and divert packages), paddles, and address stamps or codes. The part of the R&D assignment I was surprised to work with, but enjoyed immensely, was voice activation. After I became an expert in voice activation, I was asked to present it to visiting managers. One day, some executive managers of the company, some of whom were reported to be on the board of directors, attended my presentation on voice activation. After my presentation, one of the managers asked me how long I had been learning this specialty. I replied I was in my fourth month. They were blown away. The funny thing is I was trying to dumb down the vocabulary during the presentation to prevent "speaking over their heads."

Then something happened that opened my eyes wide to the importance of computers and automation. A young man joined our team as a new college graduate—I will call this person Mike. Mike worked almost exclusively with the company's corporate manager who oversaw IT—I will call him Max.

One day, I asked Max what Mike was doing with us. He explained how he was helping us program the automation to make it all work together smoothly. I asked Max why he needed someone like Mike since his own ability and knowledge was far superior to everyone else in the company. Max said, "Mike makes me look like an intermediate student. He will run this portion of the company one day." My eyes bulged out of my head after hearing this statement. I realized if this person was so important to our company, which had hundreds of thousands of employees, then computerization and automation really is the future of business.

Recently, as the operations manager of a construction company, I had several challenges to overcome, one being to find a way to automate my inventory. I knew from experience that there are ways to place barcodes or labels on equipment so it can be scanned by a laser and placed into the computer inventory program. When I asked my owner why we were not doing this, he told me to speak to another manager about it. I spoke to the other manager, Oscar, about how this automation of inventory would increase efficiency and minimize errors. He said the main challenge was pasting labels in a place where they would not be damaged on stop signs, construction signs, etc. A solid idea came to me after learning this, but I did not offer it due to his continued comment. Oscar said, "Besides, the owner will not make the investment because he doesn't see the value." This was the craziest thing I have heard in quite some time. We were using employees to count the inventory on a monthly basis. We paid multiple employees to work multiple hours to count all the products and equipment. We were willing to continue wasting this money on a monthly basis every month for years, but we did not want to invest in automation. Yet all of us managers received calls concerning our employees' hours that were too high. I think this is where the saying "Truth is stranger than fiction" applies.

My son explained to me how he could create a program where the inventory would interface with the active job program. This would inform the company how much each of the satellite operations had in inventory and how much inventory was on each jobsite. Then he would program it so each manager in the company (or only the owner if he wished) could see how much equipment was at each location and what was available for relocation to another jobsite. The program would keep track of cost, reorder needs, and shortages and would reduce the cost of counting inventory monthly.

I finally asked my son to go ahead and write a program to automate as much as he could. I told him to act as if he oversaw the company. He wrote a program to perform the following functions:

1. Automate inventory (in yard and on-site)
2. Automate active jobs (color coded to highlight completed and upcoming jobs)
3. Automate payroll
4. Calculate revenue and cost per job (this would interface with P&L statement)
5. Calculate equipment on each jobsite (this would interface with the billing department)

This automation would save me a great amount of time, which I could use to call customers, train supervisors and foremen, learn more about one of our division's processes, take a computer class, or any other important matter.

My son (Thomas) showed me a website he completed during college. It was far above our company's website. Today, many project managers who take over companies are younger people who grew up with the internet. When several young managers called and told me they found us via the internet, my first concern was the image they had of our company's generic, nonimpressive website.

Thomas also determined why we were experiencing so many issues with our e-mail system. It was due to our failure to use the proper software with our server. These issues were causing loss of service, resulting in customer complaints. It was causing managers to waste time trying to fix these issues, which further induced and increased stress and anger within the company. The bottom line is that the outdated technology being used was costing the company money, reputation, and headaches. Thomas explained that the communication issues between the software and server we faced were caused by incompatible software systems. I asked him to further explain, until I understood what he would do differently. He simply responded that he would use the same server and software so they would communicate properly.

My son was willing to sit down with the owner of the company and explain what could be done to automate his company in a cost-effective way, the costs that would be saved, and whom he should hire and what to pay them. My son was not interested in the position since he was studying for medical school, but the owner was not interested in this investment. My son showed my manager and the son of the owner of the company what was possible. They both liked the ideas he had and the self-made programs he showed them, but the owner was not willing to consider it. Yet he was upset every time the e-mail system went down or managers did not turn in their inventory on time. He was upset when payroll was turned in late or billing was not done correctly. Do yourself a favor, use computers and automation properly to increase the efficiency and profits of your company.

The owner was not understanding or willing to consider automation. He was not open-minded. If automation saves your managers time, they will have more time to work in areas of their strength instead of wasting time and people on administrative duties. We were stepping over thousands of dollars to pick up a nickel.

If you are in business today and your company is not automated, you have two options: get on the train or be left behind.

21

Sales and Marketing

> You will get all you want in life if you help enough other people get what they want.
>
> —Zig Ziglar

Everyone is in sales. Everyone is a salesperson. I have a relative Connie, who said she could never do sales or marketing. I asked her why she felt this way. She explained she did not like when people tried to sell her things; therefore, she could not enjoy selling to someone. I asked her if she felt she could market products or services. She reminded me she did not like doing sales. I quickly realized she considered marketing and sales the same job. I decided to have some fun and explained she had done both jobs at dinner that evening.

Over the years, I have asked many friends, family, and employees what they see as marketing and what is sales. Most people do not know the answer to this. The response I usually get is that sales is selling someone something they do not want. I usually laugh for a bit before I can gather my serious side to explain that this is the wrong idea. I also explain the difference between marketing and sales. An easy way to remember the purpose of marketing and sales is this:

Marketing is creating a need. A sale is fulfilling a need.

Yes, this is simplistic, but it is true and an easy way to separate the two. Marketing is creating a need that may or may not exist. When Thomas and Alicia (my son and daughter) were in middle school, I explained this definition to them using refrigerators as an example. I asked them how many homes they have been in which did not have a refrigerator. They said every home has a refrigerator. I explained how companies that sell refrigerators did a great job, when electricity was still a novel invention, of creating a need for refrigerators. My kids both stated how refrigerators were necessary and made good arguments to support their position. I appreciated their deep thought and conviction on this matter. I then asked them two simple questions: "When were refrigerators invented? What did people do before refrigerators were created?" I explained how refrigerators did not exist prior to electricity in the form we have them today. I reminded them there are still many people throughout the world today who do not have a refrigerator. I went on to explain how people historically used to dig holes in the earth or use cellars in homes to keep certain nonperishable foods cool. Items we keep in the refrigerator today, such as milk, eggs, juice, meat, cheese, etc., were often made or harvested daily. When people needed milk, they would milk a cow or goat. When they needed eggs, they would take them from the chicken nests. Juice was pressed from fruits like apples, oranges, pineapples, etc. Coconuts were punctured or cut open to get milk. Meat was derived from a fresh killed animal. People would cook the rest of the meat they could not eat or wrap it well and store underground to keep cool. Sometimes they would dry and cure the meat to make jerky.

Once my kids realized refrigerators were not necessary, although they did not experience life without one, they started to understand *marketing*.

The first thing marketing does is create awareness. Let us say you are starting a new business and you are confident that potential customers do not know where you are located or what you offer. In this case, you market your business. Marketing tells the purchaser where you are located: "The first three rules of marketing are location, location, and location." This shows the importance of making people aware of your company. In addition to knowing where you are located, people need to know what you do, when you are open, how to contact you, and what you provide, service, or produce. Most importantly, marketing should tell consumers how they can purchase your product or service.

The biggest result of marketing is creating a need. Marketing tells the consumer why they need to have this product or service. In the 1970s, a popular marketing ploy for Coca-Cola was the television commercial that endorsed, "Have a Coke and a…smile." If something absolutely, positively had to be there the next day, FedEx told you to "FedEx it." If we wanted something "mmm good," we needed a Campbell's soup. Today, McDonald's sells, "I'm loving it." Folgers informs us "the best part of waking up is Folgers in your cup." All these ads are attempts to remind us of a need we have. The message tells us how their product is available and satisfies this need.

Signs (or shingles as they were called) were used as the first form of marketing outside of a storefront many years ago. This informed a person riding by on horseback or horse and buggy what the store offered. The next major media source was newspapers. Marketing and advertising grew once again when radio was created. Television brought us moving-picture ads and sing-along jingles that cemented into your head. Today, the internet is creating yet another source of advertising and marketing. When is the last time you went on a website that did not have at least one ad? Tough to remember, isn't it?

Marketing tells us a company exists and what their product or service is. It creates the awareness. Once marketing accomplishes this, it then creates the need. It is one thing to know of a product, but for you to buy it, you must realize why you "need" it. Thus, marketing creates the need by the message it tells you. Refrigerator marketers told us we needed their convenient and labor-saving product. It would allow us to keep food items for a longer period, reducing wastes and money needed to buy that item daily. When is the last time you walked into someone's home (in the United States), and you did not see a refrigerator? The marketers have done well. Fridges are such a convenience to have and one that we like so much, we do not want to and think we cannot live without. It truly is not a need but a nice convenience. Today, younger generations, including my children's, believe we *need* a refrigerator, as if it is a life necessity. I do not believe I need one, but I would not want to do without one.

Remember this simple point: every person in your company, including yourself, is a walking billboard. I have suggested to every company that I have been a part of to offer company T-shirts to every employee. Who does not wear T-shirts to stores, beaches, gas stations, ball games, concerts, and even church or other places of worship at times? People wear T-shirts everywhere. Not everyone wears a hat, and not everyone takes a coffee mug out of the house. T-shirts turn your employees into walking billboards, which advertise or market your business. I cannot tell you how many times I have worn a company T-shirt in public and have garnered some attention or question about it. They ask where we are located and how long we have been in business. Often, some people have remarked they did not even know the company existed. This makes me smile. Now they know who we are, where we are located, what we offer, how long we have been in business, and why they should call or e-mail us. Winner winner chicken dinner. It is a win-win: your employees appreciate the free shirt, and you get to write it off on your taxes as advertising. In this case, you may have to change the chicken dinner to a steak dinner.

Sales are fulfilling a need. Again, I enjoyed hearing my kids' perspectives when they were young, elementary school-age, on what sales meant to them. They (Thomas and Alicia) said it was selling something for less money. I asked them about higher-priced items like cars or chocolate. Then they said it was getting rid of something you did not want. I asked them who does not want chocolate or cars? Their answers had me rolling in laughter. They then said it was getting rid of something to make money. Lastly, Thomas said it was making more money without working. I was selling pharmaceuticals at the time. I left the house by 5:00 a.m., drove two hours to work, and returned home by 6:00–7:00 p.m.; so I about fell off my chair laughing at this response.

I then asked my kids if they would pay me 25¢ (a quarter) for a piece of cheese. They both said no since they had some in the refrigerator. I asked them if they would pay me $100 for my one-year-old Chevy Blazer truck. They both said yes without hesitation. I asked them if they would give me $15,000 for the same Blazer. Thomas said yes if he could get a loan. Alicia asked me if I would just give it to her. I laughed and told her she just used a great sales technique—directly ask for their business. I reminded both the reason I would be able to sell them my Blazer because they both have a need for it. They did not have a Blazer, and they wanted one. My offer filled a "want" they had. I reminded them how a sale satisfies a need. Likewise, I explained if neither of them wanted or needed the Blazer, there is a good chance I would not be able to sell it to them. There would be no need to fill. However, I explained I would try to sell them on buying the Blazer by offering them it for a cheaper price than I would sell to someone else. My son felt this was a great idea, and he was all in.

Since we have established that sales fill a need, determining if there is a need is the next step. This step is what separates a good salesperson from an average salesperson. The best and quickest way to find out if the person you are attempting to sell has a need is to simply ask them how you can help them. You can follow up with other questions: Do you own one now? What do you like about this product? Would you want it in a certain color? What features do you have now?

I remember calling on a urologist, who I knew would not be interested in my sales pitch. He had so many reps calling him trying to sell their medication. I knew he would approach me with contempt, so I devised a different approach. Instead of telling him about the great benefits of the drug I was selling, I would ask him what qualities a drug would have if he produced it. When I asked this question, his eyes refocused on me. He stated the drug he made would be (1) safe, (2) efficacious, and (3) inexpensive. Therefore, I used this order when presenting my sales pitch of the drug to him. When I was done, he said he would try it. I was so shocked; I almost questioned him since I was so used to him saying he would think about it. Remember, sales are as much listening as it is talking. In many cases, it takes more listening than talking.

Speaking of physicians, this recalls a key to success in sales: *persistence* with a positive attitude and sharing humor will achieve more results than talent alone. One day, while I was a pharmaceutical representative, I arrived at a hospital at 7:00 a.m. I set up my table, brochures, donuts, apples, and pens with the company name on them. The first physician arrived at about 7:15 a.m. and asked me if he was right in remembering I lived in a town two hours away. I told him he had a good memory. He asked me if I stayed in a hotel last night. I explained I was home the night before to attend events my kids had, so I left home at 5:00 a.m. to get to the hospital by 7:00 a.m. to meet him. When he reminded me that the snow was coming down heavy and it was blowing like crazy, I joked, "The company doesn't pay me for my intelligence, Doctor, just my persistence." We both laughed and continued a great sales exchange. Persistence will get you the success you need and the respect of those you call on.

Getting back to my relative Connie, whom I mentioned in the beginning of the chapter, I explained how she marketed and sold earlier this night. She asked me how she did so. I asked her if she remembered telling us about the plants she bought for her yard, to which she said yes. I asked her if she told us where she bought them, and she admitted she did. I explained she just did some marketing for this company as she made us aware of the company that sold quality plants and where this company was located. She almost apologized for doing this. I told her she helped us, and I was going to tell that plant company what a great marketer she is.

I asked her if she remembered asking us if we needed any plants. We agreed we did need new plants, so I then asked what kind of prices the company was offering. I pointed out that she asked if we had a need and told us we should go to that company for that need. I told her she is a bona fide salesperson. She resisted for a moment by stating she was not selling anything for the company but was just trying to help us. I told her every representative should *sell to help* the consumer, and the great ones do this. When you help the customer, you help the company. When you help the company, you help yourself. This is what separates a great sales rep from an average rep. Therefore, the good salespeople ask many questions before selling—they want to make sure they get you what you are looking to buy. They understand if they can help you fulfill your need, they have a better chance of making the sale. I asked my relative how much she would charge me to hire her to train other sales reps. She smiled and said, "Oh no. I'm really not a salesperson." I told her not to worry; everyone is a salesperson when he or she wants something.

I explained how husbands sell wives on why they need to be home at a certain time to watch the sports game. Wives sell husbands on why they had to buy a product because it was on sale now and they needed it anyway. Kids sell parents on why they should be allowed to go see a movie with friends. Parents sell kids on why they need to be in bed on time for their health or to think clearly in school. I told Casey that Alicia wants me to give her my Blazer. I told her how Thomas would buy it so he can flip it for a profit. We laughed about their quip remarks and responses to what sales and marketing are, and I teased her for a while on her newfound skill as a sales rep.

The one point about sales you must always remember as a business owner or manager is *sales is the only function that brings money into your company*. All other departments and functions cost you money. Therefore, you must hire, train, and reward the best salespeople possible. It is also a reason a business owner needs a good sales manager.

I will get into what it takes to be a top-tier sales representative in my next book. I was in the top 7 in a company with a sales force of five thousand representatives. In that book, I will share many of the secrets I learned in those four and a half years of selling. I can tell you now one of the keys to sales is humor.

The last basic aspect of sales I will share with you for now: WIIFM (What's in It for Me from chapter 9). When a salesperson is selling a product or service, they will tell the potential buyer about the company, product, and features of the product. As a potential customer listens to your spiel, they wonder, *What's in it for me?* It is vital to tell them what they will gain or benefit from the product or service. This reminds them of something they do not have that will help them. This reminds them of something they need or want fulfilled. This is necessary in every attempted sale you make. It is one of the most important factors to enable a buyer to understand you are helping them. Instead of the buyer buying something you are selling, they are buying something they need. You just helped them obtain it.

I will never forget what President Albert T. Annexstad said to us in his only meeting with us new employees for his company, Federated Insurance Company. Federated Insurance was the fastest-growing midsized insurance company in the country at the time. Al started as a sales representative and earned his way to the top as president. He told the class I was in that one of the first things he did to grow the company was to make the three division managers face each other. He literally asked all three to move their desks to the middle of the building and face the desks toward each other. He then told his division managers they needed to work together to grow sales and make the company more successful. Did it work? Well, it grew the business faster than before, and the employees all enjoyed the success. Al went on to say that everyone, including himself, was a salesperson. I am proud to say I won the new employee award in my class, which was voted on by the instructors and students. My picture was placed in the company's board of directors meeting room.

Today, Federated Insurance Company remains a top-performing company (Wikipedia):

> In 2013 Federated Mutual Insurance Company and Federated Life Insurance Company were named to the 2013 Ward's 50® groups of top performing insurance companies. Federated is one of only two organizations that

has had affiliated companies named to both the property-casualty and life-health Ward's 50 group of companies every year since 2001.

Today, the company is led by CEO Jeff Fetters. In 2003, Jeff, VP at the time, spoke to the new employee class, which I was a part of, about the importance of our job to the customers and policyholders. He explained in excellent detail how we, as marketing representatives, positively affect the lives of our customers through our insurance policy. Everyone in class, without any exception, believed that Jeff would become the next CEO of the company, which unraveled as expected. It was apparent that he was highly professional, polished, intelligent, and caring. Today, Federated Insurance deserves to be at the top of their industry due their long legacy of great leadership.

22

Leading the Good (People, Product, and Service)

Always put people first, for without them there is no organization.
—Amit Kalantri

Why does your business exist? Most business owners reply to this question: it exists to provide a needed service or product to others or society. *How* does your business exist? The answer most business owners provide is simple: good people.

You're a good person. You started your company, or you are a manager in a company. You are a leader. Many people want to avoid the challenges that come with owning a business. Especially with the bureaucracy we have today and the licenses, taxes, insurance, fees, EPA, FTC, IRS, DOT, and other agencies, running a business is like walking through a maze. You are taking this challenge head-on, and you have the courage it takes to be successful. Thank God if you have the desire, ability, persistence, and attitude to become a leader. The principle of primacy says, "What we learn first, we learn best and retain the longest." God, or whomever is your higher power, is first. We place trust in Him or Her to guide us.

Remember, when you find an employee (laborer, foreman, supervisor, manager, or executive manager) who is willing to work and do what they can to be successful, work diligently with them. I have seen too many companies fire or lay off employees who thoroughly wanted to work with the company. They made good relationships within the company and were liked by others. Often, they had abilities in certain areas, but the company fired or lay off the employee because they were not as good as another employee in another area. Let me share a scenario for emphasis.

When I was an operations manager for a construction company in Florida, I wanted to hire an employee who had a variety of mechanical experience. (The owner of the company suggested I hire an employee with less mechanical background so that he or she would receive less pay.) My area of responsibility was six hours wide and two hours deep of drive time. I agreed that a mechanic would help reduce the expenses of trucking damaged fleet and equipment back and forth. If the owner of a company "suggests" something, do it (unless it is unsafe or illegal).

Now, the person I hired (I will call him Roger) did not have formal certifications or training to show on his behalf. However, I knew from having friends' dads who were excellent mechanics without certificates that Roger could still perform very well for the company and fulfill the position's needs. When I asked Roger what kind of mechanical background he had experienced, he gave me examples of where he worked and what kind of work he provided. He had worked in a bus garage, where he learned from a friend how to repair buses and large trucks. He also had worked in a car garage with another friend, where he learned how to repair cars and pickup trucks. I asked him to describe some of the work he performed. Roger explained that he repaired engines, chassis, breaks, radiators, bumpers, etc. Basically he could repair and rebuild everything, except transmissions or major body repair. His response pleased me greatly since these were the only two kinds of repair the company's owner wanted going to the home office. I hired him, and in a year's time, Roger saved the company tens of thousands of dollars. I received a call approximately one year after successfully running this operation. How successful were we running? The owner showed me the P&L (profit and loss) statement, which reflected that I increased revenue by $584K the first six months of the year compared to the first six months of the previous year, while also reducing expenses 1.7 percent. We also grew our safety results from eleven months with no injuries to two years. Every category improved.

Therefore, as you might guess, I was shocked to hear my owner wanted me to fire or let go of Roger even though he was doing a great job mechanically. The owner informed me Roger caused an accident when he tried to move around a stopped van during a traffic jam five months earlier. The van had twelve or so people inside, who said they were fine the day the accident occurred since the accident occurred at such low speeds. However, several of the van's occupants later filed a lawsuit stating they were injured. I called the owner when the accident occurred several months earlier, and we agreed I would take him off the road from driving to jobsites and direct him to work on other projects. He would remain as our yard equipment repairperson and mechanic. Now, I am getting a call to fire him, which I was able to prevent from happening by highlighting how much Roger helped the company. I always say when you find a good employee who wants to work hard and do a good job, do not fire them. Find a place where this person can be successful. There are employees who do the minimum and do not care about the company, so when you do find someone who has talent and cares, keep him or her. Rodger was successful at fixing vehicles, which saved us service time, money, and stress as it prevented work from backing up. He went on to be a particularly important cog in the wheel. Later, some of our corporate mechanics were terminated. This resulted in too few mechanics to keep up with their own work, let alone the amount of work required by the satellite office fleet. Roger was able to handle all our fleets' needs and keep me from having to ship trucks and equipment weekly, eight hours round trip.

I advise to find a place for good, hard workers like Roger. Roger wanted to work, he performed excellent mechanical work, and he cared about the crew and his job. I managed to keep Roger, and I am glad I did. Apparently, the owner was happy I did also. Roger is still working there today, and I am not.

23

You Want the Nuggets

> All that is gold does not glitter.
> —J. R. R. Tolkien

The California Gold Rush (1848–1855) began on January 24, 1848 when gold was found by James W. Marshall at Sutter's Mill in Coloma, California. (Wikipedia, 2015)

The Gold Rush was said to have drawn three hundred thousand people to California in search of their fortune in gold. These people were after the golden nugget since they saw that each nugget brought more wealth and a better future.

I believe you will find the same result when you implement these gold nuggets while operating as a manager or new business owner. My wish is that even a veteran business owner will be reminded of something they have forgotten since they first started their business. Someone wiser than I once said, "It is not what we learn in life, but what we remember, which will make us successful." I hope you remember some of these simple business practices to assist your company to great success:

1. God first and ask for guidance.
2. The three important people to start your business are the banker, attorney, and accountant. Keep them close to you.
3. Pinpoint the kind of people you want in your company, then attract, train, and retain them.
4. Train people properly and never stop training.
5. Communication is a huge challenge. Get better, daily.
6. Safety—make it a personal value. It is more important than service or production. Safety training builds trust, and trust is vital to success.
7. Do not fear failure.
8. Allow the great people you hired to give input and create good for your company, as well as for themselves.
9. Care—it is what will push you and your company to the top 1 percent.
10. Follow up—it is where success is reinforced or lost.
11. Maintain one goal—it allows for more creativity in achieving it. Too many goals box in thinking to the one goal and take away from the main goal. If one has too many different goals, it may be easy to accomplish one goal, but this will cause one to lose sight of the others. Having one goal allows you to be creative in designing many ways to achieve it with less restriction.

12. It is difficult to become number 1 in customer service and number 1 in cost reduction. The cost–benefit ratio will assist you. Just remember to take care of the customer.
13. Accountability—how do you reward without it?
14. Discipline is necessary, but only after proven training.
15. When you have accomplished the first goal, do not forget to celebrate. Have fun.
16. Setting a new goal—let your people set the new goal. They will attain it. You will have to work as a guide or leader in this process.
17. Burnout—prevent it by allowing people to set goals and hold everyone accountable to perform, not just a few. Understand everything has a law of diminishing return.
18. Ego—take it off at the door, or just cage it away. Tame it before it kills you.
19. Leaders—when you find a good one, keep him or her. When someone cares, all you must do is mentor him or her.
20. Allow leaders to create and lead. Stay out of the way, or fire them and you do their job. It does not make sense to pay them and constantly change what they are doing.
21. Mentoring—it is your succession plan. It is the future of your leadership and success.
22. Persistence—do not ever give up. Keep going and you will learn how to overcome challenges.
23. People—it is how your business exists. Even in the day of computers and robotics, people still program and maintain the automation. Choose the right people. Train the right way. Reward and inspire through leadership. Allow for creativity and celebrate your people. Success is yours before you even count your profits.
24. It is about "more than you"!

My wish is for each of these gold nuggets to bring you success and prosperity. I have learned quite a few things by implementing and following these nuggets in business practice. My experience has told me that you can make a positive difference in your employees' lives, and they will return the favor. My business experience has led me to believe that leaders will be knocking down your door to join you. My experience tells me you can lead your industry in safety, service, and production, resulting in your accountant providing you with exceptionally good news.

The gold rush begins now: grab your gold nuggets and put them to use.

Regardless of your beliefs, please remember one thing when you become successful: you are not God. You are successful because of God. God is within you, and you two are unbeatable together. You are successful because of the good people whom you choose to help you and work with. Do not let the ego kill your success. Attract and hire talented people. Train correctly from day one and never stop training. Continue to communicate and establish a process to make sure all levels of the company receive the same message. Recognize and reward good employees. Promote those who put the employees and your company first. As the leader, keep learning and keep an open mind. Near lastly, do not forget to laugh. We all make mistakes. Find the humor in every moment, and you will feel the weight lift from you. Humor invites creativity to the party. Moreover, never stop praying. Life is about "more than you."

God bless you and good leading.

ABOUT THE AUTHOR

Thomas DePetro is the youngest of eight children, proving he's a survivalist. He was born in the beautiful Upper Peninsula of Michigan in the mid-1960s.

He is in his thirty-fourth year in the business world. He has twenty years of leadership experience (management). He has been in operations, HR training and train trainers, R&D, industrial engineering, business owner, sales manager, and business development director.

He grew up in the picturesque town of Marquette, located on the south shore of Lake Superior. This made him a snow tunnel specialist. He loves the outdoors.

He was a three-sport athlete in high school and was offered a double scholarship of basketball and football after high school.

He went on to play football at Northern Michigan University, where he lettered three of four years. Several of his teammates went on to play in the NFL and left him behind.

He earned a bachelor's degree in marketing management, which offered him marketing and management knowledge.

He has a deep appreciation for the arts, which is likely brought on by his lack of artistic skills.

He loves a variety of music from classic rock to opera and jazz to clean rap. He secretly raps when no one is around.

He has started and led nonprofits and served on a few boards.

He loves people who try their best and attempt to do the right things on a daily basis. He has zero appreciation for large egos, which reduce creativity and inclusivity.

He has two beautiful adult children, Thomas Anthony and Alicia Fae.

The love of his life is Holly. He's putting her up for sainthood for putting up with him.

He loves his Lord and his God, Jesus Christ. He would need thousands of volumes of books to explain all He has done for him.

He never imagined himself as an author but found his experience in business and life presented him with information and perspectives, which others could benefit from.

He found he thrived as a coach in sports and a trainer in the business world. He truly enjoys helping others succeed: the feedback he receives is indescribable.

His only goal is to help others through his books and give Jesus all the glory.

CPSIA information can be obtained
at www.ICGtesting.com
Printed in the USA
LVHW090511030322
712522LV00002B/9